The Crisis of Color and Democracy

Essays on Race, Class and Power

Manning Marable

Common Courage Press   Monroe, Maine

Cover by Norma Whitman

Photo: Bruce Wang/RIT Communications

Library of Congress Cataloging-in-Publication Data

Marable, Manning, 1950—

The crisis of color and democracy : essays on race, class, and power / by Manning Marable

p.cm.

Most of the essays originally published between 1988 and 1991 in author's commentary series which appeared in various newspapers throughout the U.S., Canada, Europe, and India.

ISBN: 0-9628838-2-4 pbk, ISBN: 0-9628838-3-2 cloth

1. Afro-Americans--Politics and government. 2. United States--Politics and government--1989- 3. United States--Politics and government--1981-1989.I. Title.

E185.615.M279 1991

305.896'073--dc20

91-30730

CIP

Common Courage Press

P.O. Box 702

Monroe, ME 04951

207-525-0900

All portions of several essays were published previously in the following journals and magazines:

"In Pursuit of Educational Equality," *Black Issues in Higher Education,* Vol. 7, no. 25 (February 14, 1991), p. 80; also published in *NIP Magazine* (April 1991), p. 32.

"Fight Against Apartheid not Finished," *The Witness,* Vol. 74, no. 4 (April 1991), pp. 10-11.

"The Values of Manhood," *Essence,* Vol. 22, no. 1 (May 1991), p. 42.

"Multicultural Democracy," *Crossroads,* Vol. 1, no. 11 (June 1991), pp. 2-7.

"The Myth of Equality," *The Witness,* Vol. 73, (April 1990), pp. 18-19.

"The Legacy of Martin Luther King, Jr.," *The Witness,* Vol. 73 no. 2 (February 1990), p. 15.

"Beyond Academic Apartheid: A Strategy for a Culturally Pluralistic University," *Black Issues in Higher Education,* (December 7, 1989), pp. 24-25.

"Do the Right Thing," *Black Issues in Higher Education,* Vol. 6, no. 11 (August 17, 1989), p. 64.

"The Cultural Crisis in Education," *The Witness,* Vol. 72, no. 3 (March 1989), p. 22.

"Race and the Demise of Liberalism: The 1988 Presidential Campaign Reconsidered," *Black Issues in Higher Education,* Vol. 5 (December 22 1988), p. 76.

"The Politics of Division," *Christianity and Crisis,* Vol. 48, no. 18 (12 December 1988), pp. 438-440.

"The Politics of Intolerance," *The Witness,* Vol. 17, no. 10 (October 1988), pp. 6-8.

"A New Black Politics," *The Progressive,* Vol. 54, no. 8 (August 1990), pp. 18-23.

"Blacks and the Republicans: A Marriage of Convenience?" *NIP Magazine* (August 1991), p. 33.

"Toward Black American Empowerment: Violence and Resistance in the African-American Community in the 1990s," *African Commentary: A Journal of People of African Descent,* Vol. 2 (May 1990), pp. 16-21.

"Thurgood Marshall: The Continuing Struggle for Equality," *Black Collegian,* Vol. 20, no. 3 (January/February 1990), pp. 72-78.

"The Tragedy of Marion Barry," *NIP Magazine* (January 1991), p. 21.

Second printing.

Contents

Chapter III
Economic Underdevelopment
and the Contradictions of Capitalism

Chapter IV
In Pursuit of Educational Equality

Chapter V
Racism and Apartheid:
Along the Color Line

Chapter VI
America's One Party System

Chapter VII
Jesse Jackson, The Election of 1988, and the Bankruptcy of American Politics

Chapter VIII
Black Protest and Empowerment

Chapter IX
The Challenge of Multicultural Democracy

Acknowledgements

Not since the publication of my first book, *From The Grassroots,* published in 1980, have I had the opportunity to collect and edit my popular writings on politics. I began writing "Along the Color Line", a political commentary series, for African-American publications fifteen years ago. The column now reaches millions of readers weekly, and we have recently initiated a radio version of the series which is distributed to a number of stations throughout the United States. Unlike most black theorists and essayists, I regularly receive abundant feedback from community leaders, students, feminists, labor union activists, and others. These constructive and critical responses are a corrective factor in my own work, keeping me in touch with the contemporary mind and mood of African Americans. The column has permitted me to maintain a kind of praxis, theoretical engagement and practical political involvement, which is rare. My publishers and editors have been crucial in supporting the series.

Most of these essays were written during my tenure as Professor of Political Science and History, at the University of Colorado's Center for Studies of Ethnicity and Race in America. The University of Colorado has generously provided support for my research. The Center's Director, Dr. Evelyn Hu-DeHart, has always been helpful as a friend and colleague.

Over the past two years, the graduate students and undergraduates who comprise my research staff, Eleanor A. Hubbard, Brenda Rodriguez, Cher Ferrell, Ramona Y. Beal, Marcus Grant, Millicent Adu, Paul Cornelison, and Edet Belzberg have provided invaluable assistance in locating resources and information which has been useful in my work. Linda Robinson, my administrative assistant, has been particularly helpful this year in expanding the

"Along the Color Line" series to radio stations and to dozens of new subscribers. Her constant advice, including the suggestion for the book's title, has been insightful.

Greg Bates and Flic Shooter of Common Courage Press merit my thanks for suggesting the publication of these essays, and, along with Laura Reiner, for their energy and hard work throughout the summer of 1991 in producing this book.

Finally, as always, I acknowledge my greatest debt of all, to my wife, partner, and lover, Hazel Ann. Political insights are never divorced from a person's practical life experience. My own personal background and training as a scholar and political essayist taught me to analyze a problem intellectually. But the essence of an issue is seldom found solely in its narrow details. Hazel Ann's great gift is the ability to see through problems, to grasp their core, and to explain herself in a language which grassroots, working women and men can easily understand. The concerns and perspectives she expresses naturally are generally those I encounter among my black readers. As Hazel Ann likes to say, no political idea is too complicated that it cannot be communicated to black folk and working people. The challenge and burden is not on the audience, but on the writer, in the effort to be understood. And the purpose of these political essays is not simply to interpret the world, but to change it.

—Manning Marable
Boulder, Colorado, July 18, 1991

Introduction:
The Crisis of Color
and Democracy

Democracy has failed because so many fear it. They believe that wealth and happiness are so limited that a world full of intelligent, healthy, and free people is impossible, if not undesirable. So the world stews in blood, hunger and shame...Such a world, with all its contradictions, can be saved, can yet be born again; but not out of capital, interest, property, and gold...

—W. E. B. DuBois[1]

The Crisis of Color and Democracy is largely a compilation of essays written over a three-year period since the presidential primaries in the spring of 1988. Most of these essays originally were published in my commentary series, "Along the Color Line," which appears in over 200 newspapers throughout the United States, Canada, Europe and India. The style and character of these essays are greatly influenced by the political outlook and concerns of my regular readers, most of whom are African Americans. For them, institutional racism, unemployment, sexism, poverty, educational inequality, and hunger are not theoretical abstractions. The majority of black people have little faith in the altruism of their government, or in the commitment of George Bush to civil rights or social justice. Therefore, my approach in these essays does not appeal to some amorphous "mainstream," or to the goodwill of white liberals. I feel no obligation to mute the expressions of anguish or outrage ascending from America's ghettoes, which are explored in these pages. The task of "Along the Color Line" has been to present issues and political events from a progressive analysis for a largely black audience.

Although covering a wide range of topics, these essays reflect several general perceptions about the current nature of American politics and the state of the black freedom movement. The first premise is that the black struggle for equal rights in the United States was forged in a special set of domestic and international realities after the Second World War. Globally, the basic political division was the conflict between American and Western European imperialism vs. the Soviet Union and its allies. Third world revolutions and social protest movements, in Latin America, the Caribbean, Asia, and Africa were waged in a bipolar context. In some regions, naked colonial rule was forced to retreat, but neocolonialism in the form of military juntas or dictatorships was imposed in its place. In South Africa, racial capitalism initiated a brutal authoritarianism termed "apartheid." Within the United States itself, the massive migrations of African Americans from the rural south to the urban north, combined with the gradual increase of black influence within the political system, had the effect of escalating sentiments for rapid democratic change. Blacks took to the streets in nonviolent demonstrations for desegregation and civil rights. The threat of international communism and the growing drives toward independence in the third world created great domestic pressure on the federal government and corporations to make concessions. With the successful adoption of reformist legislation on civil rights, thousands of previously disfranchised African Americans entered the political process, and soon contended even for the presidency itself.

In general terms, this was the political terrain which largely helped to define the contours of African-American struggle for four decades. Even during the period of black nationalist upsurgence and political radicalism between 1966 and 1976, the basic elements outlined above set certain parameters on the character of protest movements. The political ideology, behavior and cultural consciousness of several generations of African Americans were rooted in a set of truths which were unquestioningly accepted. The ideological worldview of most African-American leaders, with the exception of the Black Power period, could be termed "integrationist." Integrationism meant the elimination of structural barriers which prohibited blacks from full participation within the mainstream of American life. Culturally, the goal was achievement of a "color-blind society," which in the words of Martin Luther King, Jr., would mean that blacks "will not be judged by the color of their skin but by the content of their character." For the integrationist, there was an implicit faith in democracy, American-style. The system could be made to work, they believed, if only people of color and others victimized by discrimination and poverty were brought to the table as full partners. This could be realized by expanding the number of African Americans, Latinos, women, low-income people and others into positions of authority within the existing structures of power in business, labor, government and the media. When one encountered resistance, the integrationist strategy relied heavily on the intervention of a "benevolent" federal judiciary, which could be counted on to defend civil rights and civil liberties. Internationally, integrationists sympathized with the anti-apartheid struggle, but they failed to grasp the fundamental linkage between the battle against racism abroad and their own situation within the United States. Most failed to comprehend how the existence of a strong communist bloc internationally pressured the United States to make various political concessions to democratic protest movements domestically. For example, the Soviet Union's polemical attacks against America's system of racial segregation were important in pushing the Kennedy and Johnson administrations toward liberal reforms on civil rights.

Politically, integrationism in the period 1954-1988 largely accepted the premise that the electoral system was both rational and inherently fair. Political inequities existed only when certain classes of voters were arbitrarily barred from exercising the right of franchise, or prohibited from running for office. With the passage of the Voting Rights Act of 1965 and other civil rights legislation, all members of society supposedly had an equal access to the process of democratic decisionmaking. The central flaw of this political reasoning was the fact that democracy is only really possible when all the participants have roughly equal resources as they enter the electoral field of competition.

Both major political parties had a vested interest in "managing" if not eliminating the electoral participation of blacks, the unemployed, low-income workers, and others. In national politics, the Republicans had become by the 1980s an upper-to-middle-class white united front, for all practical purposes. Two-thirds of all whites, and three-fourths of all upper-class whites voted for Reagan in 1984. The Republicans saw few advantages in encouraging the electoral participation of constituencies which were highly inclined to vote Democratic. But the Democrats also had problems with black and low-income voters, for several reasons. Increased black electoral clout would be translated into organizational influence within the Democratic Party's structure, which would shift the ideological axis of the part to the left. Most white Democratic officials were convinced that the Democrats had to move to the right, incorporating elements of the Reagan agenda into their own programs. Consequently, throughout the 1980s the actual influence of African Americans as a group declined within the mainstream of both parties.

The years 1988 through 1991 brought an end to the political certainties which had characterized the previous four decades. The most striking transition occurred within international politics. The massive internal con-

tradictions within Eastern European nations finally culminated into a collapse of Stalinist communism. Inside
the Soviet Union, oppressed national minorities challenged the legality of the central government; longtime
dissidents such as Andre Sakharov and rebel former communists such as Boris Yeltsin denounced Marxism-Lenin-
ism with popular approval. The demise of the Marxist
political system drove many third world countries into a
new accommodation with western imperialism. Within
Europe, the collapse of the communist Left set the environment for a resurgence of ethnic violence and racism.
In France, the new fascist sentiments of the National
Front were absorbed into the major capitalist parties. In
the Netherlands, the Centrum Party which advocated
discriminatory policies against nonwhites was formed; in
England, the Thatcher government warned that it would
not permit the island nation to be "swamped by people
with a different culture." The eastern capitalist nations
moved swiftly to implement policies checking the emigra-
tion of Arabs, Asians, Africans and other nonEuropeans.

Inside the United States, the renaissance of racism
assumed several distinct new forms. In the wake of the
civil rights movement, it was no longer possible or viable
for white elected officials, administrators and corporate
executives to attack "niggers" openly. The Ku Klux Klan
and other racist vigilante groups still existed, but did not
represent a mass movement among whites. Instead a
neoracist strategy was devised which attributed the
source of all racial tensions to the actions of people of color.
David Duke, former Nazi and Klan leader, received the
majority of whites' votes in his Senatorial race in Louisiana by arguing that "affirmative action" programs discriminated unfairly against innocent whites. Black
college students were attacked as "racists" for advocating
the adoption of Black Studies academic programs, or the
creation of African-American cultural centers. Black
workers were accused of racism for supporting special

rain people of color in supervisory and admin-
positions. In this context, "racism" had begun to
as any behavior by individuals or groups which
empowered Latinos, African Americans or other people of
color, or an agenda which took away long-held privileges
of white elites. Of course, the concept of "reverse discrimination" could only exist if African Americans, Native
Americans, Latinos and other people of color actually
controlled institutional resources which could affect
whites' life chances and opportunities. If they owned the
banks and financial institutions, the systems of transportation, communication, housing and health services, even
commensurate with their percentages of the population,
then one might theoretically perceive a pattern of institutional prejudice aimed at whites. But of course, this is
absurd. White, upper-class males still retain a thousand
different advantages over virtually any person of color,
from private schools and special tutorials to prepare for
standardized tests for admission to colleges and professional programs, to membership in private clubs and
access to capital from financial institutions. Even at their
best, affirmative action plans and programs barely dented
this entrenched pattern of power, privilege and elitism
which the upper class terms "meritocracy."

Ronald Reagan was unquestionably the fountain-
head of much of the new racism. His administration was
openly contemptuous of African-American rights; he nominated virtually no people of color to the federal courts,
and openly supported the apartheid regime abroad
through his policy of "constructive engagement." George
Bush pursued the presidency in 1988 by employing
Reagan's racial strategy. His campaign cited the infamous
example of black convict Willie Horton as an example of
Democrats' "softness on crime." Without open appeals of
white supremacy, he nevertheless benefited from a racist
backlash against the gains achieved by racial minorities
since the 1960s. As president, Bush continued to pursue

this racist agenda while employing a public style and discourse of racial harmony. He openly courted black middle-class leaders, inviting them into the White House, and spoke at historically black colleges. He publicly endorsed the passage of a civil rights bill, so long as it repudiated affirmative action and other effective measures to reduce discrimination. With the resignation of Thurgood Marshall from the Supreme Court in June 1991, Bush immediately nominated another African-American judge to replace him. But Bush's choice, former black nationalist-turned-Reaganite Clarence Thomas, was a vicious opponent of affirmative action, women's rights and civil liberties. Thomas was so conservative that he had even criticized the crucial *Brown v. Board of Education* decision of 1954, which had abolished racially segregated public schools. Yet the National Urban League refused to take a public position against Thomas's nomination. The NAACP was also silent until pressure from other liberal constituencies forced this organization to oppose Thomas on ideological grounds.

The reason for the absence of strong resistance to Bush's efforts to undermine desegregation and to Thomas's nomination to the court was, in short, the bankruptcy of the ideology of racial integration as practiced by the African-American middle-class leadership. If one argues that the elevation of increased numbers of African Americans or other people of color into positions of public prominence will automatically expand black political power, then the nomination of Clarence Thomas to the Supreme Court would be perceived as a "positive" political gesture, regardless of his political ideology. One could even assert that it was preferable to have a black, Latino or woman conservative, rather than a white affluent male with the same political views. This sort of "symbolic politics" in effect permits the white corporate political establishment to select its own "minority leaders," such as Linda Chavez, Thomas Sowell, Shelby Steele, and

Thomas, who have virtually no constituencies among people of color and who vigorously reject affirmative action and civil rights. Since the vast majority of African-American community-based leaders have little to no access to the media, little dialog really exists between working-class and inner-city black communities and representatives of the white elite. Of course, no dialog is really being sought by the latter; the object is to "manage" the unpredictable and volatile urban masses of blacks, Latinos and the unemployed, by elevating small numbers of nonwhites into positions of authority. The contemporary crisis of liberalism was also apparent in 1990-1991 with the U.S.-orchestrated war against Iraq. The invasion of Kuwait by Saddam Hussein had little to do with the actual behavior of the American government and military. After all, when Israel launched its invasion of Lebanon less than a decade ago, the U.S. government did virtually nothing. In the post-Cold-War era, with the Soviet military abandoning its posts in Eastern Europe, an "external threat" was needed to justify the billions of dollars allocated for American conventional and nuclear weaponry. The casualties of hundreds of thousands of Iraqi civilians were required to secure American access to cheap energy supplies. Despite the anti-Arab racism and chauvinism which was generated by this unnecessary conflict, most liberal groups, white and black, did nothing to halt it. Most trade unions and the NAACP were almost silent. Despite efforts from students' groups and the fragmented Left to initiate demonstrations and public protests of various kinds, those who opposed the Gulf War were largely isolated. The absence of liberal opposition to the conflict meant that the media and politicians were successfully able to protect a "national consensus" for war.

But probably the best example of the bankruptcy of liberal politics, at least in the context of the African-American electorate, was the phenomenon of "post-black politics." The weight of ideological conservatism, the destruction of affirmative action and the electoral triumphs of Reaganism in the 1980s, led many black liberal politicians to attempt a type of decentralization. They knew that the black community was deeply hostile to Reaganism, and that if they continued to run for public office within a black district or constituency they must advocate progressive viewpoints. Yet in order to move up with the electoral system, to run for statewide offices or for the U.S. Senate, black liberals would have to appeal to white, middle-to-upper-class voters who traditionally supported Republicans. Thus in the 1980s, a tendency emerged among black leaders which sought to appeal to a more centrist audience. Rather than denying the reality of race, these post-black politicians tried to "transcend" the racial boundary by talking about colorless economic and social issues. The best example of the post-black politician was Virginia Democrat Doug Wilder. In his successful effort to gain election as his state's first African-American governor, Wilder moved sharply to the right. Once a strong opponent of the death penalty, he suddenly embraced capital punishment. Wilder repudiated his earlier support for Washington, D.C. statehood, and distanced himself from Jesse Jackson.

Compounding the sense of political crisis and the failure of liberalism within the African-American community was another dilemma of even greater dimensions. This second crisis can be characterized by a deep sense of fragmentation and collective doubt, rooted in group consciousness and social existence. The symptoms of this internal crisis were the widespread drug epidemic, black-against-black violence, the growth of urban youth gangs, and the destruction of black social institutions. By the late 1980s, about 12,000 African Americans were being murdered annually. For young African-American males in their twenties, the murder rate was more than one in twenty. Such violence inevitably spread to the character of social relationships. People concerned with street violence, the danger of robbery or death, would be reluctant to attend neighborhood political meetings after dark. Black-owned business in the central cities lost patrons and support, making it even harder for small entrepreneurs to survive. Churches and community centers located in crack-infested areas found it difficult to attract many middle-class African Americans. Large sections of major cities such as Detroit were depopulated, as hundreds of thousands of black working-class and middle-income people fled to the suburbs. Much of this internal crisis within contemporary black life must be understood against the backdrop of corporate and governmental decisions, which deliberately called for the underdevelopment of the ghetto. Millions of higher-paying industrial and manufacturing jobs fled the central cities in previous decades, as corporations liquidated their assets and relocated to nonunionized, low-wage states and countries. With the collapse of the economic infrastructure in America's urban centers, and the failure of the federal government to initiate an economic reconstruction program, the illegal economies of crack and crime became the only means for the survival of many people.

The Rainbow Coalition of Jesse Jackson represented the only viable alternative in national politics to both the growing trend of semi-Reaganism within the Democratic Party, and the accommodationist currents of "post-black" politics among ambitious black Democrats. Unfortunately, despite the mobilization of millions of voters and the articulation of a progressive economic and social program, the Rainbow Coalition failed to live up to its full promise. Part of the problem was the absence of organization, the failure to establish a national publication or training schools for local organizers. Jackson himself was temperamentally opposed to launching a formation which he did not control, and he fought the democratic election of local Rainbow leaders and the initiation of activities which undercut his authority. But the real problem was neither with Jackson's personality, nor with the organizational inefficiency or chaos of the Rainbow. The unresolved question confronting Jackson and the Rainbow Coalition was whether the Democratic Party could be transformed from within, as an effective vehicle for the aspirations of the poor, working people, racial minorities and others. What became strikingly clear in the Democratic Party presidential primaries of 1988 was that the idea of internal realignment was an illusion, and that activists themselves would be the ones "transformed" by advancing a theory of change resting solely on the electoral system. Many Rainbow activists, as well as thousands of young black community-based leaders, had forgotten some of the most valuable lessons of the black freedom movement.

For politics to be relevant again, we must perceive ourselves in a period of transition, and to think of activism in a new way. This means, in part, the initiation of new organizations and institutions of collective struggle. Local activists could start "freedom schools" in community centers and churches, bringing together young people with veterans of trade union, black nationalist, and radical protest movements. A new approach to politics must revive "older" techniques, such as economic boycotts of corporations which do not have strong affirmative action policies, or civil disobedience against symbols or offices of government repression. This also must mean the cultivation of long-term dialogs and greater understanding between progressive groups, rather than the type of transitory coalitions which predominate in left politics. At the heart of this strategic rethinking must be a Latino-African-American alliance on a wide range of issues such as housing, health care, education, job training programs, affirmative action, and fairness in the criminal justice system. As long as strategic cooperation and discussions between Latinos and African Americans are delayed, especially at the neighborhood and community level, the fragmentation and manipulation of both groups will continue by both major parties. In effect, we must go well beyond the notion of the Rainbow Coalition as a pressure group within the Democratic Party. We must launch the protracted process of building an alternative political apparatus, with people of color at its core, which is fully committed to participatory democracy and full equality, in both the political and economic senses of the term.

The old political ideologies, strategies and organizations no longer can advance the boundaries of progressive change, within the African-American community. We are between the old system of Jim Crow institutional racism, and the beginnings of what can become a genuinely pluralistic, multicultural democracy, in which African Americans, Asians, Arab Americans, Latinos, Native Americans, women, lesbians, gays, working people, and others who have experienced oppression are at last fully empowered. This collection of essays is both a critique of what has gone wrong in American society and politics, and a projection of what might constitute a transitional strategy to reestablish the democratic struggles of oppressed people on a firmer foundation. The most difficult task of political change is to perceive issues and problems in a new way, turning what might seem to be difficulties into opportunities for advancement. Our generation's task is to build upon the protest traditions of the past, without becoming imprisoned by that history and the limitations of the vision of its leaders. These essays suggest, hopefully, an approach to politics which can one day uproot institutional racism, sexism and all forms of human inequality, while establishing the parameters for a democracy which truly represents all the people.

NOTES

1. W.E.B. Du Bois, *Color and Democracy: Colonies and Peace*, Millwood, NY: Kraus-Thomson, 1975, pp. 99, 142.

Chapter I

The Black Community from Within: Cultural Identity and the Social Crisis

Wiping Out
the Spirit of Resistance

Whenever I have lectured before a large audience in recent months, inevitably I am asked the same question. Essentially, it goes something like this: "The black community is in the midst of an unprecedented social crisis. Unemployment, bad housing, reductions in health care and education programs, police brutality and other factors are undermining the social stability of black neighborhoods. Given the state of affairs, why aren't Afro-Americans rioting in the streets? What is keeping a check on black urban militancy, when the material and social conditions which gave rise to the riots of the 1960s are actually much worse today?"

There is no precise chemistry which can reliably predict the creation of an urban explosion, even though critical volatile elements are currently present. But social discontent and rage can be channeled away from meaningful public protests into purely self-destructive activity. The energy and dynamism of black urban youth may be manipulated for destructive and self-defeating purposes.

The struggle against illegal drugs is being lost in most of this country's major inner cities. Recent federally-financed studies state that the major group which has turned off from drugs such as cocaine in the past five years is the well-educated, white upper middle class. Many hispanics, blacks, low income people and those with less than a high school education have continued and/or increased their collective drug dependency. The crack epidemic continues in poor urban communities virtually unchecked. In one recent study of heroin addicts in New York City, it was determined that blacks and hispanics comprised about 75 percent of all the city's addicts. An-

14

other 1982 survey of data on drug dependency, based on material from over 30,000 treatment centers, showed that 44 percent of all addicts were black; 20 percent were hispanic, and only 36 percent were white.

There was no recognized "drug problem" in this country until the crisis of illegal drugs began to claim thousands of victims among the daughters and sons of the white upper middle class. As long as cocaine was identified with black musicians, street people and/or prostitutes, no real social problem was said to exist. Recent data illustrate that illegal drugs not only serve to diffuse black collective action for development; but that also the drug issue may receive less governmental and media attention as its victims become once more predominantly black and poor. As Dr. Mitchell S. Rosenthal, head of Phoenix House, a network of drug treatment centers, states: "In the heroin crisis of the late 1960s and again with crack in recent years, it was the threat to the middle- and upper-middle-class kids that put pressure on legislatures and Congress. There is a danger that if they feel less of a threat, the resources won't stay with the problem."

Another continuing problem for blacks, as well as other Americans, is alcoholism. There are conservatively an estimated six to nine million confirmed alcoholics in the U.S. Blacks, essentially those with lower levels of income and education, have a disproportionately high rate of alcoholism. There's also evidence that alcoholism is a rapidly growing problem for black women. Statistically, most black women are more likely not to drink alcohol than are white females. However, the proportion of heavy or "problem drinkers" among black women is about three times the proportion of white females classified as heavy drinkers.

There is also growing evidence of an unprecedented rise in the suicide rates of blacks, especially younger blacks since the civil rights era. Between 1950 and 1977, for instance, the annual suicide rate of black males soared from 6.8 per 100,000 to 11.4 per 100,000. Also in these years, the black female suicide rate more than doubled, from 1.6 per 100,000 to 3.5 per 100,000. Nearly one-half of all suicides among Afro-Americans occur today among young adults, between the ages of 20 and 34. Within the more narrow age group of 25 to 29, the suicide rate among black males is higher than that for white men and women living in urban areas, whose suicide rate is also higher than the white average. Why are black young adults killing themselves in record numbers?

You don't need an occupying army to wipe out a spirit of resistance among any oppressed people. You simply pump unlimited supplies of cocaine, heroin and other drugs into their neighborhoods. You burden them with an unemployment rate of 20 percent and higher. You give them poor schools, few health clinics, and reinforce white corporate standards of beauty and materialism in the media and popular culture. Drug dependency, alcoholism and suicides are the logical result. The worst manifestation of oppression is that which is generated internally, not externally.

September 1987

The Myth of Equality

The American economic and political system promises equality, but has never delivered for the African American. In fact, the system uses the rhetoric and myth of equality to hide the process of oppression. Both through legal and illegal means, blacks are being destroyed.

Illegal drugs destroy thousands of African Americans in many direct and indirect ways. We witness the daily, destructive impact with the proliferation of gangs and fratricidal criminality. But there are other indirect effects as well. In January 1990, a comprehensive study by the New York Hospital-Cornell Medical Center, which reviewed traffic fatalities from 1984 through 1987, observed that nearly one in four drivers age 16 to 45 killed in New York tested positive for cocaine in autopsies. Researchers suggested that individuals addicted to cocaine experience spatial misperception and other physical dysfunctions. How many thousands of African Americans are crippled and killed in accidents caused by those whose abilities are impaired by crack or other drugs? How many homes are destroyed, and dreams shattered? How many daughters and sons are lost forever from their families and friends?

The cancer of crack creates many more living victims than those who are killed by the drug. Crack is part of the new urban slavery, a method of disrupting lives and "regulating" the masses of our young people who otherwise would be demanding jobs, adequate health care, better schools and control of their own communities. It is hardly accidental that this insidious cancer has been unleashed within the very poorest urban neighborhoods, and that the police concentrate on petty street dealers rather than on those who actually control and profit from the drug traffic. It is impossible to believe that thousands and thousands of pounds of illegal drugs can be transported throughout the country, in airplanes, trucks and automobiles, to hundreds of central distribution centers with thousands of employees and under the so-called surveillance of thousands of law enforcement officers, unless crack represented, at a systemic level, a form of social control.

Most African Americans do not realize that the most destructive drug problem within our community is tobacco addiction. The tobacco industry makes its highest profits from African Americans. For two decades, tobacco companies have followed a strategy of "special marketing," targeting younger, poorly educated African Americans as potential consumers. In late December 1989, for example, R.J. Reynolds Tobacco Company announced the development of "Uptown" menthol cigarettes, a product specifically designed to "appeal most strongly to blacks." One NAACP leader has called the strategy "unethical," and the American Cancer Society has declared that the "campaign exploits blacks, especially the ghetto poor."

It should not be surprising, therefore, that African Americans currently suffer higher death rates for virtually all types of cancer, especially cancer of the lungs, prostate, esophagus and cervix, than white Americans. The statistical life expectancy for blacks actually *declined* in the late 1980s, due in part to extremely high mortality rates from cancer.

However, the major means for the social control of the African American remains the criminal justice system. As of June 1989, the U.S. prison population reached 673,000, of which blacks comprise 46 percent. Prisons have become the method for keeping hundreds of thousands of potentially rebellious, dissatisfied, and alienated black youth off the streets. There is a direct correlation between the absence of job training programs and social programs designed to elevate blacks' incomes, and the increased utilization of the criminal justice system to regulate unemployed and unemployable blacks. Keep in mind that between 1973 and 1986, the average real earnings for young African-American males under 25 years fell by 50 percent. In the same years, the percentage of black males aged 18 to 29 in the labor force who were able to secure full-time, year-round employment, fell from only 44 percent to a meager 35 percent. Is it accidental that these young black men, who are crassly denied meaningful employment opportunities, are also pushed into the prison system, and subsequently into permanent positions of economic marginality and social irrelevancy? Within America's economic system, a job has never been defined as a human right; but for millions of young, poor black men and women, they appear to have a "right" to a prison cell or place at the front of the unemployment line.

The struggle against the myth of equality requires a break from the tactics and ideas of the desegregation period of the 1960s. Our challenge is not to become part of the system, but to transform it, not only for ourselves, but for everyone. We must struggle to make economic and racial equality for all.

February 1990

Black Against Black Violence

The urban ghettoes of America increasingly are becoming armed, military zones. Millions of people live in fear of being raped, robbed or mugged. Thousands of homes are burglarized every week in black neighborhoods. Hundreds of our young people are being slaughtered in the streets and back alleys. And many of our high schools are now battle grounds for drug pushers.

Between January and August 1988 — only eight months — 143 people were murdered in Miami, a figure which was higher than the city's total number of murders in 1987. Crime statistics from other cities are equally grim. During the same period in 1988, New Orleans recorded 216 murders; Houston, 411 murders; Washington, DC, 323 murders; and New York City, 1,231 murders. The vast majority of the victims are nonwhite males.

Urban violence frequently takes its casualties from the innocent bystanders, those who have no role in drugs, crime or murder. Two weeks before this Christmas, a nine-year-old boy died in a Chicago public housing project because paramedics refused to enter the apartment building at night. The paramedics later claimed that their ambulance was being hit by rocks and eggs hurled by local residents. The family of the dead boy disputed these charges, and filed a $60 million suit against the Chicago Fire Department. Whether the paramedics were attacked or not is secondary to the larger issue of the pervasiveness of urban violence. When postal workers, delivery workers, medics, and other health care professionals are afraid to enter entire neighborhoods without police protection, then the quality of life for the population in that area must deteriorate.

Police argue that most of the recent violence is directly attributable to the proliferation of crack. The street trade in crack cocaine is so profitable that many gangs are now as heavily armed as police SWAT teams. Witnesses of drug-related crimes often disappear; the arrests of thousands of young people who are low-level dealers has done little to keep thousands more from taking their places.

The flood of violence, however, can only be understood by going beyond the single issue of drugs. Why does violence become the sole method for resolving conflict between so many young black men? What is the long-term political and economic impact of violence within the national black community? People resort to violence in their relations with each other when they devalue the humanity and dignity of those individuals with whom they are in conflict. Disagreements are inevitable within all societies. But when people are routinely shot for less than ten dollars, or a young black man in Detroit can be murdered on a city bus for no reason, a very disturbing level of human alienation and social decay has been reached.

Black leaders must begin to address, squarely and forthrightly, this crisis of human values within our communities. Many social institutions such as churches and schools no longer exert the moral and social influence among younger blacks. The economic crisis of poverty and unemployment directly contributes to the violence as well. When people cannot eat or clothe their children, they will steal to survive. When crack dealers pay unemployed teens hundreds of dollars per day, why should they aspire to hold sub-minimum wage jobs? A person without a job and who has been influenced by the rampant materialism of the dominant culture can be recruited into criminal activity.

The only long-term, fundamental solution to the violence between black people is found within the strategy of community and group empowerment. People who are involved in political change, economic development and community-based reform movements do not destroy each other. They channel their energies into the constructive acts of socioeconomic and political change, and their outlook on their friends, peers and neighbors also changes. They seek to build local institutions and to equip others with the tools for political and social involvement, and in doing so, their understanding of interpersonal relations deepens.

If a person hates himself or herself, and has no appreciation for the culture and sacrifices of black people of previous generations, he or she will act in a criminal manner against other blacks. To end the violence, we must organize ourselves from within.

January 1989

Violence and Crime
in the Black Community

Violence in the African-American community has become an epidemic, which no longer shocks or surprises us. Year after year, the carnage and terror become worse. Last year, 433 killings occurred in Washington, DC alone, up from 369 murders in 1988. Over 1800 were killed in New York City. New Orleans, Philadelphia, Charlotte, Kansas City and other cities broke their records for homicides.

To understand the impact and devastation of violence within the African-American community, we need to review some basic facts. Violent crime, or aggressive offenses which do violence to human beings, consists of homicide, forcible rape, robbery, and aggravated assault. Property crimes, or the unlawful seizure of others' property, include burglary, larceny, arson, and motor vehicle theft. There are many other types of offenses which are defined as criminal behavior — including vagrancy, public drunkenness, illegal gambling, prostitution and embezzlement — but the most devastating types of crimes are those in which violence is committed directly against individuals, or in which a person's property is seized by force.

According to the *Sourcebook of Criminal Justice Statistics* for 1981, the total number of Americans arrested was nearly 9.5 million. Blacks comprise only 12.5 percent of the total U.S. population, but represented 2.3 million arrests, or about *one-fourth of all arrests*. Black arrests for homicide and non-negligent manslaughter were 8,693, or about 48 percent of all murders committed in the U.S. For robbery, which is defined by law as the use of force or violence to obtain personal property, the number of black arrests was 74,275, representing 57 percent of all robbery arrests. For aggravated assault, the number of African Americans arrested was 94,624, about 29 percent of all arrests in this category. For motor vehicle theft, the number of blacks arrested and charged was 38,905, about 27 percent of all auto theft crimes. Overall, for all violent and property crimes charged, blacks totalled almost 700,000 arrests in the year 1979, representing nearly one-third of all such arrests.

One of the most controversial of all violent crimes is the charge of forcible rape. Rape is controversial because of the history of the criminal charge being used against black men by the white racist legal structure. Thousands of black men have been executed, lynched and castrated for the imaginary offense of rape. Yet rape or forcible sexual violence is not imaginary when African-American women and young girls are victimized. In 1979, there were 29,068 arrests for forcible rape. Black men comprised 13,870 arrests, or 48 percent of the total. Within cities, where three-fourths of all rapes are committed, blacks total 54 percent of all persons arrested for rape.

The chief victims of rape are not white women, but black women. The U.S. Department of Justice's 1979 study of the crime of forcible rape established that, overall, most black women are nearly *twice* as likely to be rape victims than white women. The research illustrated that in one year, about 67 out of every 100,000 white women would be rape victims; but the rate for black and other nonwhite women was 115 per 100,000. In the age group 20 to 34 years, the dangers for black women increase dramatically. For white women age 20 to 34, 139 out of 100,000 are rape victims annually. For black women the same age, the rate is 292 per 100,000. For attempted rape, white women are assaulted at a rate of 196 per 100,000; black women are attacked sexually 355 per 100,000 annually.

There is also a direct correlation between rape victimization and income. In general, poor women are generally the objects of sexual assault; middle-class women are rarely raped or assaulted, and wealthy women almost never experience sexual assault. The statistics are clear on this point. White women who live in families earning under $7,500 annually have 500 percent greater likelihood of being raped than white women who come from households with more than $15,000 income. The gap is even more extreme for African-American women. For black middle-class families, the rate of rape is 22 per 100,000. For welfare and low income families earning below $7,500 annually, the rate for rape is 127 per 100,000. For attempted rape, low income black women are victimized at a rate of 237 per 100,000 annually.

Rape is almost always intra-racial, not interracial. Nine out of ten times, a white rapist's victim is a white female. Ninety percent of all black women who are raped have been assaulted by a black male. Sexual violence within the African-American community, therefore, is not something "exported" by whites. It is essentially the brutality committed by black men against our mothers, wives, sisters and daughters. It is the worst type of violence, using the gift of sexuality in a bestial and animalistic way, to create terror and fear among black women.

The form of violence which most directly impacts black men is homicide. Nearly half of all murders committed in any given year are black men who murder other black men. But that's only part of the problem. We must recognize, first, that the homicide rate among African Americans is growing. Back in 1960, the homicide rate for black men in the U.S. was 37 per 100,000. By 1979, the black homicide rate was 65 per 100,000, compared to the white male homicide rate of 10 per 100,000. In other words, a typical black male has a *six to seven times* greater likelihood of being a murder victim than a white male.

The chief victims of homicide in our community are young African-American males. Murder is the fourth leading cause of death for all black men, and the leading cause of death for black males age 20 to 29 years. In the 1990s, more black men will kill each other than the total number of American troops killed during the Vietnam war. Today in the U.S., a typical white female's statistical chances of becoming a murder victim are one in 606. For white men, the odds narrow to one chance in 186. For black women, the odds are one in 124. But for black men, the chances are one in 29. For young black men living in cities who are between ages 20 and 29, the odds of becoming a murder victim are greater than one in 20. Black young men in American cities today are the primary targets for destruction—not only from drugs and police brutality, but from each other.

The epidemic of violence in the black community raises several related questions. What is the social impact of violence within our neighborhoods? What is the effect of violence upon our children? And most importantly, how do we develop a strategy to reverse the proliferation of black-against-black crime and violence?

Violence occurs so frequently in the cities that for many people, it has become almost a "normal" factor in our daily lives. We have become accustomed to burglar alarms and security locks to safeguard our personal property and homes. More than one in three families keeps a gun in their home. We might try to avoid driving through neighborhoods where crack houses are located. We are trying to avoid the problem, but we're not taking steps to solve it. We need to keep in mind that in most of the violent crime cases, the assailant and the victim live in the same neighborhood, or are members of the same household. Half of all violent deaths are between husbands and wives. Many others include parents killing their children or children killing parents, or neighbors killing each other. There are hundreds of murders among blacks for the most trivial reasons—everything from fighting over parking spaces to arguing over five dollars.

Black men are murdering each other, in part, because of the deterioration of jobs and economic opportunity in our communities. For black young men, the real unemployment rate exceeds 50 percent in most cities. Overall jobless rates for black men with less than a high-school diploma exceed 15 percent. High unemployment, crowded housing and poor health care all contribute to an environment of social chaos and disruption, which create destructive values and behaviors.

The most tragic victims of violence are black children. Black children between the ages of one to four have death rates from homicide which are four times higher than for white children the same ages. According to the Children's Defense Fund, black children are arrested at almost seven times the rates for white children for the most serious violent crimes and are arrested at more than twice the white rate for serious property crimes. More than half of the arrests for African-American teenagers are for serious property crimes or violent crimes. For instance, the arrest rate for black youth aged 11 to 17 for forcible rape is six times higher than for whites. In terms of rates of victimization, nonwhite females are almost 40 percent more likely than white females to be raped, robbed, or become the victim of other violent crimes.

How do we understand the acts of violence committed by children? We have to begin by focusing on the concept of identity. What is identity? It's an awareness of self in the context of one's environment. Identity is based on the connections between the individual and his or her immediate family and community. We don't exist in isolation of each other. We develop a sense of who we are, of who we wish to become, by interacting with parents, friends, teachers, ministers, coworkers and others.

Our identity is collective, in that it is formed through the inputs of thousands of different people over many years. If people relate to an individual in a negative manner, an anti-social or deviant personality will be the result. If a child is told repeatedly by teachers or parents that she is stupid, the child will usually do poorly in school, regardless of her natural abilities. If a child is told that he is a chronic liar and untrustworthy, he eventually will begin to lie and steal. If she is physically beaten by her parents frequently and unjustly, she will learn to resort to physical violence against others. If a boy witnesses his father using violence against his mother, he could later become violent against women. People are not born hateful or violent. There's no genetic or biological explanation for violence or crime. Violence is learned behavior. The destructive and negative expectations projected on youth can create criminal behavior years later.

Violence between people of color is also directly linked to the educational system. If the curriculum of our public schools does not present the heritage, culture and history of African Americans, if it ignores or downgrades our vital contributions for a more democratic society, our children are robbed of their heritage. They acquire a distorted perspective about themselves and their communities. If they believe that African-American people have never achieved greatness in the sciences, art, music, economics or the law, how can they excel or achieve for themselves? Despite the many reforms accomplished to create a more culturally pluralistic environment for learning, most of our public schools are in the business of "miseducation" for people of color.

For example, Sonia Nieto's research on children's literature illustrates that the number of children's books on Puerto Rican topics or themes has dropped significantly since the early 1970s. Less than three-hundredths of one percent of all children's books published between 1972-1982 were on Puerto Rican themes. Books on purely African-American themes—not integrated topics—comprised less than one percent. African-American and

Latino book publishers are usually unable to crack the lucrative public school textbook market. Black and hispanic topics are usually taught in white public school systems as peripheral or secondary themes, and virtually never integrated across the disciplines. This type of miseducation contributes to negative and anti-social values among young people of color. If all that our youth have to measure themselves by are the distorted images of the media—the African-American male as a potential criminal, for example—then anti-social behavior will be the logical result.

We also tend to identify the issue of violence solely with males, yet an increasing number of young African-American women are caught in the cycle of drug abuse, anti-social behavior and crime. According to the research of Laurence French, between 1960 and 1974, the rate of women incarcerated in prisons increased four times faster than the imprisonment rate for males. A disproportionately high percentage are black and Latina women. For example, in North Carolina's prisons, two-thirds of all female inmates are black. Ninety-five percent of all black women prisoners have a high-school education or less. Sixty-five percent of all African-American women and about one-third of all white women prisoners have an eighth grade education or less. The vast majority of black women who are jailed earn less than $10,000 annually, are unemployed and/or are welfare recipients. In short, there's a direct correlation between inadequate or poor education, unemployment, poverty and crime.

January 1990

The Crisis of the Cities

Everybody tells you that American cities are in a state of financial and social crisis. The evidence seems so overwhelming that alternative arguments aren't even heard.

In Philadelphia, the city government has been operating with a deficit for two years. This September, a major bank withdrew its support for part of a loan, leaving officials predicting that the city would be insolvent within weeks. Mayor Wilson Goode balks at demands by state officials to increase taxes, because this would only increase the exodus of Philadelphia's middle class to the suburbs.

Detroit's population has declined from 1.8 million thirty years ago to barely one million today. Vast sections of the inner-city are plagued by crack, drive-by shootings and crime.

But the greatest outcry about the urban crisis focuses on the city many Americans love to hate, New York. Two thousand residents of that city are murdered each year, and hundreds of thousands more are the victims of rape, burglary and robbery. Violence increasingly seems to become a way of daily life. Last year, New York police officers confiscated over 16,000 weapons, only a tiny fraction of the firepower in the hands of criminals. This month, New York governor Mario Cuomo called for the appointment of an additional 5,000 cops. But the grisly death of a Utah tourist who was murdered in a New York subway trying to protect his parents from a robbery was, for many, the final blow. *Time* magazine's cover story projected New York as a metropolitan mess, an urban disaster zone of sin and debauchery. Fifty-nine percent of all New Yorkers polled claimed they would "leave the city" if they only could.

Little noted was the articulate rejoinder by the city's much-maligned mayor, David Dinkins. "Our creativity in meeting the challenges of urban America has been severely limited, not by the will of our people," the mayor noted, "but by the painful withdrawal of the federal and state governments from American urban life." Dinkins denounced what he termed the "national cleavage between rural and urban America."

Dinkins' explanation was correct, but didn't go far enough. The United States is fractured by race and class. About 40 percent of all Americans live in central cities. They are disproportionately black and hispanic, frequently unemployed or marginally employed. Their public transportation systems are failing, their schools aren't properly educating their kids, and crime is so bad in many neighborhoods that people are fearful of going out after dark. But should we blame the victims, or understand the root causes for this crisis?

The Republican Party largely writes off the cities in its political equations. The GOP caters to the interests of the largely white suburbs. The cities in the Rust and Snow Belts remain heavily Democratic, but since 1968, only one Democrat has been elected to the White House. Urban policy atrophied, as conservative federal officials told cities like New York to "Drop dead." Now the political chickens are coming home to roost. Crack dealers who terrorize black and hispanic teenagers in central cities are finding their way into the suburbs. Massive poverty and unemployment reduce America's overall productivity.

The Reagan-Bush strategy for addressing urban problems was essentially medieval—let's build a walled fortress surrounding the golf courses, shopping malls, private schools and tennis courts of white upper-middle-class society. But as the Census of 1990 reveals, the cities' problems will continue to assume a critical role, precisely because the size of the core urban populations, African Americans and hispanics, will double in the next 25 years.

Despite the loss of urban populations in Detroit and elsewhere, cities continue to be the vital centers of art, music, finance, and education. Cities are the examples of both the worst and best aspects of any civilization. What's needed is a domestic Marshall Plan for the nation's central cities. Instead of spending $300 billion next year for military weapons, we should strengthen domestic security by using our resources to build public transit systems, improve schools, establish health clinics and create jobs in cities.

October 1990

Do the Right Thing

Long before the making of "The Color Purple," the image of Afro-Americans in film had frequently sparked political polemics. The basic reason for this is quite apparent from an analysis of America's cultural hierarchy. Black Americans have long been applauded as entertainers and jesters, marginal players on the cultural stage. They may be praised for their physical grace and athletic ability. Yet when the Afro-American artist steps from the shadows into the light, and speaking in uncompromising terms, reveals through the creative arts the harsh reality of black life, he/she becomes an aesthetic pariah. Perhaps the sixties represented an exception to this general cultural rule, a fleeting moment when the Negro was in vogue. White middle-class America would rather be entertained with myths than be told the truth about race relations.

The most recent victim of the American backlash against socially-relevant art is Spike Lee, a 32-year-old black filmmaker. Lee's latest work, "Do the Right Thing," is his third film. His two previous films also focused on black-oriented themes, but did not evoke a fraction of the controversy of his current film. "Do the Right Thing" was inspired by the brutal death of Michael Stewart, a graffiti artist who was killed by New York transit authority officers for allegedly resisting arrest. The events of Howard Beach, New York, in which several Afro-American men were assaulted and one killed by a gang of whites, further crystallized Lee's concerns about the deteriorating state of race relations in America's largest city. Lee's purpose was not to produce "art for art's sake," but to create a thought-provoking and graphically honest account of racial tensions.

The essential storyline of the film is as follows: Based in a black and hispanic neighborhood in New York's Bedford-Stuyvesant area, the events take place during one hot day during the summer on one city block. Lee presents a series of characterizations of black low-income people, undereducated and jobless, but with a real sense of dignity and humanity. The characters include two black elders, excellently portrayed by Ossie Davis and Ruby Dee; Bugging Out (Giancarlo Esposito), the local neighborhood's activist who is upset by the lack of black ownership in the community; Radio Raheem (Bill Nunn), a huge young man with an equally large ghettoblaster; Smiley (Roger Smith), a young man with a speech defect who nevertheless represents the most politically advanced character in the entire film by his advocacy of the ideas of Malcolm X and Martin Luther King, Jr.; and Mookie, played by Lee himself, an unmarried father who works at an Italian-American-owned pizzeria in the heart of the black community.

The central antagonism develops when Bugging Out complains to the owner of the pizzeria that there should be photographs of prominent African-American artists, athletes and political leaders in the shop almost exclusively patronized by blacks and hispanics. When the owner refuses, Bugging Out organizes a small boycott which leads to a confrontation. Radio Raheem's ghettoblaster is smashed by Sal, the owner, and a fight ensues. The police are called and in typical fashion respond by choking Radio Raheem to death. Mookie leads the outraged residents to attack and destroy the pizzeria.

Let's focus first on the main elements or themes which Lee is attempting to explore here. Metaphors abound in the movie. Unintentionally, by projecting Smiley as a stutterer who sells photos of Malcolm and Martin, the film seems to say to us that the legitimate voices of resistance and activism in our communities are frequently held down or denigrated. There's a dialectical tension underscoring the whole film from beginning to end between a hope for interracial peace and nonviolent change vs. the need for group solidarity, empowerment and an advocacy of armed self-defense against racist brutality. This is the reason for Lee's use of Public Enemy's "Fight the Power" and the National Black Anthem, "Lift Every Voice and Sing" at the opening of the film, and the quotations from Malcolm and Martin at the conclusion.

Politics and power are at the heart of the film. We are shown black men and women who are out of work or marginally employed, living in neighborhoods which are controlled economically by nonblacks. The police treat African Americans with contempt, functioning like an occupying army in enemy territory. One is struck by contemporary parallels to Palestine or perhaps the bantustans of South Africa. To ensure the property, businesses and lives of white occupiers, the police make selective examples of nonwhites through the utilization of extreme coercion. Thus Radio Raheem's execution is not accidental, but typical of a larger question of white political domination and black oppression.

"Do the Right Thing" also presents the contradictions of black-white relations by examining the personal ambiguity between the white store owner Sal (Danny Aiello), his two sons and Mookie. The film graphically depicts the extreme racism of one son who defines blacks as animals, yet Sal is proud of his establishment and his cordial relationship with most patrons. Mookie initiates the looting of the store after Radio Raheem's death, yet the morning after, Sal is prepared to pay his former employee twice what he is owed. The reason that the film strikes a responsive chord here is because race relations *are* complex, not simplistic. Whites who are profoundly racist frequently can hate an entire group of people yet make exceptions in their relations with individuals. Sal's failure isn't personal, it's political. Bugging Out doesn't want to marry Sal's daughter, or to force him to sell the pizzeria. He only wants Malcolm's and Martin's pictures on the pizzeria wall as symbolic of recognizing the heritage and humanity of the patrons. Sal's refusal is fundamentally the refusal of white racism to recognize that human rights go beyond property rights.

A number of confused critics, black and white alike, have deplored Lee's film for glorifying violence. Journalist Juan Williams has complained that the movie "lacks vision" and promotes racial confrontation. Such criticism misses the entire point of the film. What white America needs is not a black version of Disneyland or MTV, but some insight into the social consequences of institutional racism, poverty, generational unemployment, and police brutality. If the critics spent one day in the neighborhood depicted in Lee's film, they might wonder why Lee understated the fundamental economic and social inequities experienced by residents of the inner city. "Do the Right Thing" provides a complex and dynamic examination of the state of American racism and race relations.

July 1989

Discovering "Black Manhood"
by Learning
from Black Women

Young black men are often given conflicting and contradictory messages as they are growing up. In a society which is racist and sexist, the journey of self-discovery is filled with many detours. For myself, the odyssey since my youth has meant challenging the half-hidden assumptions and values which were part of my development.

Growing up in a black, middle-class, suburban household in the sixties, my consciousness as a male was molded at first by my parents and the political environment of the times. From my father, I absorbed the values of hard work, independence and determination. From my mother, a public school teacher, I was given the gifts of spiritual strength, caring for others, and a passion for scholarship and writing. My parents' sacrifices were part of a larger, predetermined plan to make their son into a scholar.

What I learned in this secure and middle-class environment was that life was normally rational and predictable. Knowledge was power, and any problems blocking one's path could be conquered by analysis and hard work.

Most of my young male counterparts also held other stereotypes about what it meant to be a "successful black male." A strong black male never showed his feelings, or at least wasn't supposed to. He was assertive, opinionated and eminently self-confident. He knew where he was going, and was certainly in a hurry to get there.

This cardboard characterization of "manhood" was unfortunately popularized in the sixties by academics and activists alike. In college we studied Daniel Patrick Moynihan's controversial theory of "black matriarchy," which placed the blame for the disintegration of the black family and the "castration" of black males on the black woman. From the streets, our generation of young black men learned that effective political leadership was the province of males alone. One very prominent black nationalist even asserted that the only position for women within his organization was "prone." Although the crudely blatant sexism of these attitudes and remarks always turned me off, like most young African-American males, I absorbed consciously or unconsciously many of their assumptions.

The beginnings of my reconstruction as a black man began in 1974, with my appointment as a faculty member at an all-women's institution, Smith College, in Massachusetts. I became friends with a number of articulate and brilliant women who lived and worked in the area at the time. Johnetta Cole, then an anthropology professor at the University of Massachusetts, was like an older sister, inviting me into her home and shaping my nascent political ideas. The poet Sonia Sanchez inspired me to write; educator Johnnella Butler challenged me to understand the role of culture in political life.

What was most influential for me was the recognition that black women's experience had produced a set of values and perceptions which challenge stereotypes. Black women, like their brothers, have been victims of institutional racism, and understand its impact. But like all women, they also understand the oppression of sexual discrimination, and the importance of making connections between the dynamics of poverty, race and gender. Sisters have taught me to listen to the poetry within ourselves, to capture and express one's inner beauty as part of our political and social being. The nexus of beauty, warmth and strength within black women taught me to redefine my understanding of power and social change.

My most important relationship which developed, however, was with the woman who would become by wife, Hazel Ann Harris. Walking home from my new office one sunny afternoon in the early fall, I encountered a group of black graduate students talking in front of their apartment building. My eyes were drawn immediately to just about the most attractive woman I had ever seen: a chocolate brown complexion, thin and tall build, an expressive, warm face and smile, crowned with an afro rivalling Angela Davis's. When Hazel Ann opened her mouth to talk, I could hear the strong accents of Georgia as clearly as if Ray Charles himself was singing.

It was not until after we were married, two years later, that I began to realize just how different Hazel Ann's assumptions about life were from my own. She was born in rural Georgia, in a proud but poor household. Her parents had been divorced when she was an infant, and her mother always had a hard time making ends meet. Life for Hazel Ann had never been easy, predictable or fair. Instead of attending debutante balls, she picked cotton in the fields. The schools she attended were segregated and unequal.

It was from this environment of racism and physical poverty that my wife developed a perspective which has been the head and heart of countless generations of African-American women. As a child, she learned that there was nothing inevitable or logical in life. People blessed with talent and intelligence could be robbed by racism, poverty and the lack of opportunity. So Hazel Ann based her decisions on what she still calls "mother wit," the bedrock of common sense drawn from practical experience. She wasn't afraid to show her feelings, or to challenge authority.

I have witnessed and grown from these values of strength and courage in my wife. As hard as her life had been, it could not have prepared her for the murder of her brother Michael, in late 1977. Michael had been a police officer in her hometown, and after a series of harassments was gunned down by a white man. Barely four years later, her 19-year-old cousin was lynched in a wooded area outside town. Having the courage to deal with death, to find within the chaos and unpredictability of life, the strength to move forward, is the lasting gift Hazel Ann has given to me.

I'm convinced that the black man will only reach his full potential when he learns to draw upon the strengths and insights of the black woman. Many sisters have tried to tell us for years that "manhood" cannot be measured in material acquisitions, or by a set of mainstream, middle-class criteria which were never designed for us. Being proud and comfortable in our own culture and heritage, achieving accomplishments despite racism and obstacles the system places before us, is the best transition to realize both black manhood and womanhood.

May 1991

Racism and the Black Athlete

For generations, white athletes who excelled in any sport were described as "hard-working," "diligent" and "dedicated." African Americans who achieved prominence in sports, by contrast, were known as "natural athletes" who did not have to train rigorously for their success. Joe DiMaggio and Rocky Marciano were applauded by the media for their work ethic; Sonny Liston and Willie Mays were described as "naturally gifted athletes."

The basic racist assumption beneath these statements was that blacks were "animals," not human beings. Anyone knows that a horse can outrun any person. A gorilla is more powerful than the strongest weightlifter. To be black was to be closer to the physical world of beasts. And of course, whites who displayed physical prowess were said to have achieved these accomplishments by their mental powers.

A more sophisticated racism is evident today at all levels of athletics, as some white athletes who fail to achieve are quicker than ever to attribute their shortcomings to "reverse discrimination" policies favoring blacks. For example there's the recent case of Sandra Myers of Little River, Kansas. A former UCLA track star, she once held the U.S. record of 400 meter hurdles. But as black female athletes such as Florence Griffith-Joyner and Evelyn Ashford moved past her in the sprints, Myer's track career declined. Myers attributed her problems to "reverse discrimination among coaches." In 1987, she renounced her American citizenship, became a citizen of Spain, and joined the Spanish Athletic Federation as its new "star." Last month, Myers won the 100 and 200 meter competitions in a European meet. At the age of 30, this former American has become Spain's brightest hope for an Olympic Medal in the 1992 Games in Barcelona.

Why was Myers, who could barely speak a word of Spanish, prepared to surrender her American citizenship? In a recent press account, Myers explained: "For a white sprinter in the U.S. it's very, very difficult. It's kind of a phobia, you just don't see any white sprinters, and coaches aren't interested in developing them."

Myers argues that her race has become a liability within the United States. "The Americans have a problem because they have too much natural talent," Myers explains. "Black athletes are naturally gifted; they make great sprinters and jumpers. Why should a coach work to develop a white athlete when he doesn't have to do anything with a black athlete? They just recruit them, time them, and they have a winning team."

Myers' statements represent the "new racism" of Willie Horton bashing and Bush administration assaults on affirmative action. The argument is not only racist, it's illogical in the extreme. In reality, success by any group in any avenue of human endeavor is largely determined by the factors of opportunity, availability of resources, and the level of individual dedication.

Why do African-American athletes dominate the NBA, but are virtually unrepresented in the National Hockey League or the Professional Golfers' Association? Build five thousand ice skating rinks and public golf courses in the African-American community, and create hundreds of training programs and incentives for black elementary school children. Believe me, within twenty years you'll have some whites writing about the "natural ability" of blacks in golf and ice hockey!

Blacks excel in athletics because opportunity is still limited in professional and corporate circles for minorities and women. Expand job access and affirmative action enforcement, and fewer blacks would go into sports.

Racial discrimination is still rampant in college athletics. A recently released NCAA study indicates that the graduation rate after five years for black athletes is only

26.6 percent, compared to 52.2 percent for whites. More significantly, the vast majority of white athletes drop out of college during their early years while nearly as many black athletes leave school in their final years as in their first two. This implies that many coaches and academic officials are more concerned with eligibility rather than the goals of education and graduation, when it comes to black athletes.

The NCAA study also indicated that when African-American and white athletes have the same SAT scores, blacks graduate from college at higher rates than whites. This shows that standardized tests are a poor indicator of future academic performance, and that blacks with lower SAT scores shouldn't be arbitrarily denied admission to higher education.

Shed no tears for Sandra Myers, the little white princess who fled to Europe because she couldn't keep pace with black women sprinters on the track. The real victims of racism on the playing field remain people of color.

July 1991

Chapter II

Human Needs,
Human Rights

The Health Care Crisis for Black Americans

One of the chief legacies of the Reagan-Bush administration in the field of social policy has been a disastrous record in all matters of health care. With a callous contempt seldom equalled, the Reaganites have done everything possible to destroy the possibility of decent, affordable health care for all Americans. This assault has had a particularly devastating impact on black Americans, and upon other people of color and working people in general.

A brief review of the statistics illustrates the failure of the Reagan-Bush administration to finance programs to narrow the health status gap between blacks and whites. Blacks suffer higher death rates for most types of cancer, especially cancer of lungs, prostate, esophagus and cervix, than whites. For diabetes, the disease still remains 33 percent more prevalent among blacks than whites, and 50 percent more common among black women than white women. For hypertension, blacks still suffer two times the rate of strokes and high blood pressure than whites. In terms of infant mortality, black babies die at a rate twice that of white infants.

Why are the health care statistics for blacks so poor, despite notable efforts in the field of public health? First, the United States is one of only two industrialized, western-style countries which does not have a comprehensive, national health care program financed by the government. The only other nation without such a plan is the apartheid regime of South Africa. Consequently, millions of minorities, low-income people, small farmers, the homeless, and the unemployed cannot afford private health insurance, and they delay going to a doctor or dentist until it is usually too late. Even many middle-income families cannot afford to see a physician or dentist on a regular basis.

Access to health care facilities which provide quality services is another problem. Back in 1950, there were 200 black-owned hospitals located in black communities across the country. With the emergence of desegregation, black health care facilities began to disappear due to lack of funds. This year, there are only ten black hospitals remaining. According to Dr. David Satcher, President of Meharry Medical College, "We've got almost 40 million in this country who lack access to basic health care, and the problem is being exacerbated by the closing of hospitals that have historically taken care of black and poor people. The question is, who's going to pick up the slack as these hospitals close?"

Dr. Satcher has noted that the demise of black hospitals contributes to a growing doctor-patient ratio for minorities and the poor. The U.S. average doctor-patient ratio is currently one to 500. "But for black people in Alabama," Dr. Satcher notes, "it is probably about one to 3,000."

Racism and economic discrimination against low-income people combine to reduce the quality of life and health care for millions of nonwhites. According to Dr. Everlena M. Holmes, Dean of the School of Health Sciences at Hunter College, "Over *60,000 excess deaths* occur each year among blacks in this country." These are black people who would not have died had they received the same standard of preventative treatment, medical care and access to health insurance which the majority of whites have.

Part of the solution resides with advancing strategies to boost the number of blacks who are going into the health care professions. But Dr. Holmes has also observed that "in spite of the expressed need, the number of blacks entering (health) education programs has declined significantly since 1975. This decline is consistent with the decreased federal initiatives and support for allied health education programs and students." Dr. Holmes adds that the crisis has been compounded by the fiscal crisis of many historically black universities in recent years, which have been forced to curtail and even eliminate most of their allied health education programs. To narrow the racial gap in health care "will require the collective effort of educational institutions, the federal and state governments, and health care system, parents, the media, and allied health organizations."

September 1988

Unequal Medical Care: Race and Class Factors in Health Issues

To be black, hispanic, poor or unemployed in America means, in part, an unequal access to basic resources. The poor and jobless don't have decent housing or quality education. Our social policies are designed to perpetuate economic inequality by preserving difference in the health, education and physical welfare of classes and racial groupings within the social order.

Part of the reason for this is simply racism. For example, researchers at Harvard University recently found that a significantly higher proportion of whites who are treated at Massachusetts hospitals with heart problems undergo coronary bypass operations and cardiac catherizations than do blacks suffering from identical health problems. Similarly, blacks are less likely than whites to be given kidney transplants, even when they have the same incomes and insurance coverage. Researchers disagree as to the reasons for differences between the races in patient care and treatment. But they are convinced that "the differences were not merely a function of diminished physician contact and lower disease recognition for blacks", because the differences occurred even among individuals hospitalized for severe heart problems.

Another recent study on medical care illustrates that despite advances in the facilities and treatment of many African Americans in terms of health, there are significant differences in the frequency of access to medical facilites between blacks and whites. For instance, in 1986, 37 percent of all blacks surveyed had not visited a doctor in more than a year. The average number of visits to a doctor by whites is 4.4 per year, vs. only 3.4 per year for African Americans. Nearly five in six whites surveyed received regular blood pressure checks, while about one in three blacks surveyed had not had annual blood pressure checks. Blacks are also less likely than whites to have health insurance; they have much more difficulty in getting to hospitals or clinics than whites; and they use emergency rooms far more than whites do.

Because we don't have a comprehensive, national healthcare policy, the United States fails to support the concept of a medical "safety net" for millions of nonwhites, the poor and lower-income people. In the void of a national health insurance system, the demands of the market place dictate the medical treatment for millions of people even outside of the poverty level. Doctors tend to go into subfields of medicine in which their financial compensation will be high, and the risks from being sued are reasonably low. Rural areas have a difficult time attracting dentists and physicians, because medical professionals don't earn enough money to pay off their loans or live a comfortable lifestyle.

In some instances, the increase of certain medical procedures reflects the desire for increased profits. Back in 1975, for example, the rate of Caesarean section operations among live births was 10.4 percent. Ten years later, the percentage of Caesareans rose 22.7 percent. Today, it is 24.4 percent, nearly one out of four births. Medical doctors note that there is no medical reason why the number of Caesareans should have jumped so dramatically in so short a time. But Caesareans are more cost effective, hospitals state. They avoid the long hours of waiting involved in many vaginal births, and the inconvenience of night deliveries. More to the point, vaginal births now cost about $2,900; Caesarean births costs anywhere from $5,000 to $7,000. This economic fact alone raises the question of whether the medical interests of women and children are being served when the market is the basis of health decisions.

A central part of the agenda for black political empowerment must be to promote awareness of health care issues and strategies to reduce the medical inequality by race and class.

February 1989

Discrimination Against
the Physically Challenged

Suppose you applied for a job and were told bluntly that your physical appearance was simply too offensive and objectionable to the patrons? Or that when you waited at the bus stop, you weren't able to climb aboard? Suppose you could not obtain access to schools, churches, and most business establishments? And suppose the vast majority of Americans complained that any changes which would accommodate your concerns were well beyond the means of taxpayers?

No, we haven't returned to the era of Jim Crow, to the segregated buses and lunchcounters. We're referring instead to another form of discrimination—the segregation and prejudice against Americans who have physical disabilities.

About 43 million Americans, one out of every six individuals, are physically challenged. This includes not just people in wheelchairs or who are deaf, but also those who have epilepsy, learning disabilities, and diseases such as AIDS. The physically challenged are frequently dismissed from jobs, or are denied jobs despite their educational backgrounds or professional experience. People who contract cancer and are in treatment, for instances, can lose their jobs. Many jobs in industry or commercial establishments which do not require physical mobility or dexterity deny opportunities to those confined to wheelchairs or to amputees. And perhaps the most vicious discrimination targets those who have contracted AIDS. Instead of viewing victims with compassion, millions of Americans refuse to rent apartments or houses to people with the disease. Children with AIDS are shunned from public schools, and infants of AIDS parents frequently aren't adopted.

When many individuals suffer disabling accidents, they can be denied their full legal and human rights even by well-meaning but misguided relatives. One classic example is proved by the controversial case of Sharon Kowalski. For four years, Kowalski lived together with another woman, Karen Thompson. In late 1983, Kowalski was in a serious automobile accident which left her unable to move physically or to speak. Immediately after her accident, Thompson devoted months assisting Kowalski to relearn basic movements, and assisted her overall physical therapy. When Kowalski's parents learned of the lesbian relationship between their daughter and Thompson, they angrily refused to permit Thompson to have any access to her. Thompson responded by filing for guardianship, and a legal battle erupted.

The Kowalski case illustrates two types of bigotry—homophobia, or hatred of homosexuals and lesbians, and handicapism, the paternalism and mistreatment of physically challenged individuals. Kowalski has been denied the right to freedom of association, the right to the counsel of her own choice, and the right to be examined for competency. During last years presidential campaign, Jesse Jackson issued a statement in support of Kowalski and Thompson, which declared: "We question the wisdom of any ruling which seeks to separate mutually consenting adults who have made a life commitment to each other. Homophobia, sexism and handicapism should never again be allowed to limit the potential and abilities of any person."

The struggle for civil rights is not simply based on color and ethnicity—it is rooted fundamentally in the belief of equality for all human beings. Should physically challenged people be judged by the dominant society solely by their difference, or by the affects of a disease? Half of all Americans over age sixty five suffer from some type of disability. The struggle for equality must include the abolition of all discrimination creating a second class citizenship for the physically challenged.

June 1989

A Woman's Right to Choose

The Supreme Court's ruling on abortion sparked a major political debate across the country in recent weeks. As expected, the high court did not overturn the landmark *Roe v. Wade* decision which established legal abortions nearly two decades ago, but instead greatly curtailed the access of lower-income and unemployed women to safe abortions. By a five-to-four vote, the Court declared that states do not have to provide funds, facilities or employees for abortions, or to encourage or counsel women to have abortions. If states adopt such restrictions, this decision could affect almost all hospital abortions, which comprise about 10 percent of the 1.5 million abortions done annually.

More ominously, however, the recent abortion decision indicated that four of the nine justices were fully prepared to overturn *Roe v. Wade*. Three of the pro-choice justices are 80 years or older: William Brennan, Thurgood Marshall, and Harry Blackmun. Even if Sandra Day O'Connor, a Reagan appointee to the Court who declined to outlaw *Roe* in the recent case, doesn't join the so-called pro-life group, odds are that President Bush should soon appoint another member to the Supreme Court who holds equally reactionary views on the issue of abortion rights.

The battleground on abortion is rapidly shifting to individual states, as state legislators and governors in the 1990 elections will be examined closely by both pro-life and pro-choice groups on the abortion issue. Although most pro-choice groups are aligned with the Democrats, and the pro-lifers tend to be ideological conservatives and Republicans, the division on this controversy isn't strictly partisan. There are millions of white, ethnic Catholics in urban areas, generally working-class or blue-collar, who are morally opposed to abortion and reject the use of government funds to provide abortion to anyone. Conversely, millions of suburban, upper-class whites who are nominal Republicans on fiscal issues also hold liberal views on abortion. They reject the pro-life view that the state has the right to dictate a woman's individual decision regarding abortion. Nationally, most Americans strongly favor a woman's right to a safe abortion, and oppose the arbitrary outlawing of abortions under all conditions.

The abortion issue needs to be addressed within the African-American community, in part because pro-life groups have consistently distorted the position of blacks as being strongly pro-life. African Americans have experienced a history of being victimized by forced sterilizations and other oppressive strategies to limit or cripple our population, so it is not surprising that most blacks have political reservations about any involvement of the state in health issues.

What's striking about the abortion debate from the vantage point of the black freedom struggle is the profound ideological inconsistency of the majority of pro-life groups. They demand full legal rights for an embryo, and are willing to set aside the wishes of the pregnant woman, regardless of such factors as poverty, unemployment, the absence of a male spouse or whether pregnancy resulted from rape. Pro-life conservatives frequently don't express any interest in how a nonwhite, pregnant young woman is going to be able to feed, clothe, educate and house a child once it comes into the world. Is it fair or just to impose such a burden on teenage mothers? And given the reductions in federal expenditures for jobs, food stamps, housing and health care, the outlawing of legal abortion means the massive expansion of an underclass largely consisting of young, unemployed women of color and small children.

The black community has a direct interest in fighting for a woman's right to control her own body, and to preserve the option of safe, legal abortion as a matter of personal choice. To do less would compound the problems of poverty, powerlessness and sexism within our community.

August 1989

What is Obscenity?

In recent months there has been a series of controversies concerning efforts to censor political and artistic activities which are deemed unpopular, subversive or "obscene." The most recent conflict concerns the Supreme Court's decision to permit the burning of the American flag as a form of free speech protected by the first amendment to the Constitution. Lawmakers stumbled over themselves to denounce the five-to-four decision as antipatriotic. Senate minority leader Robert Dole threatened to use the flag burning issue against Democrats who supported the Supreme Court's ruling. Many conservative Republicans with libertarian politics, who opposed any governmental restrictions on free expression and speech, nevertheless embraced the jingoistic and dangerous proposal to halt flagburnings by passing a new Constitutional amendment.

In popular culture, the advocates of censorship have targeted the black rap group, 2 Live Crew, for the sexually explicit lyrics on its album "As Nasty as They Wanna Be." Broward County, Florida sheriffs arrested a record store owner for selling the controversial album, after a federal judge declared it to be "obscene." Several members of 2 Live Crew were arrested by authorities for performing the album's songs in an evening performance. Conservative critics demanded more than a political pound of flesh from the black artists. One angry newspaper columnist declared: "You can't package garbage and sell it as food. [Similarly], society must have the strength to say to even popular rap groups such as 2 Live Crew, 'Shut up!'"

Florida Republican Governor Robert Martinez, looking to make cheap political gains, jumped on the censorship bandwagon, declaring the record "pornography. If you answer the phone one night and the voice on the other end begins to read the lyrics of one of these songs, you'd say you'd received an obscene phone call." Even some African Americans approved of the 2 Live Crew arrests. Author Jewelle Taylor Gibbs noted: "Young people see [this music] as freedom of speech, but...it's socially unproductive." The banned record has sold nearly 2 million copies nationwide, and sales increased sharply after the group's arrest and legal harassment.

The flag and 2 Live Crew controversies raise several immediate questions. Why is 2 Live Crew considered obscene and illegal, while white performers such as Andrew Dice Clay make an affluent living promoting sexism and vulgarity while being featured on Saturday Night Live? Do you suppose that race could have something to do with the difference in treatment?

Why is 2 Live Crew arrested for singing rap songs, while another federal judge, Howard E. Cook, ruled this May that the Ku Klux Klan is a "persecuted group" and that a state ban on the wearing of masks in public illegally restricts the Klan's "free speech"? Judge Cook declared that Klan members needed "anonymity provided by a mask to exercise their First Amendment rights." This interpretation of the law assumes that the Ku Klux Klan has been the victim of political harassment and violence, rather than the reverse. This ruling turns upside down the actual history of the Klan, and in effect censors those who are the frequent victims of Klan violence.

The basic problem in the interpretation of free speech is that both liberals and conservatives do not comprehend the real meaning of tolerance. Liberals tend to believe that tolerance means the free expression of all ideas, regardless of whether they are right or wrong. Conservatives generally repress free expression. But the real meaning of tolerance is supporting ideas and values which enhance life and promote cultural and political pluralism. Ideas and expressions having a destructive character, or organizations which have long, documented histories for committing acts of terror, murder and arson, should not be permitted.

Thus the Ku Klux Klan's "right to speak" was forfeited years ago, because it has a lengthy history of racist and anti-Semetic violence. Permitting the Klan to march through a Jewish neighborhood, or to circulate membership flyers in interracial high schools, is an open invitation to harassment and violence.

But the right to burn the American flag as a free expression of one's political views about this nation, is no threat to anyone's life, liberty or personal property. Public demonstrations, picketing, civil disobedience, and symbolic protests such as flag burning are the essence of democratic political expression, and should be encouraged. Diversity in artistic expression, similarly, represents the soul of cultural pluralism. The 2 Live Crew's songs, by this standard, are certainly sexually explicit and lewd, but don't merit official censorship.

We must keep in mind that the real obscenity is not represented by 2 Live Crew, but by the fact that three million Americans are homeless and thirty million others live below the federal government's poverty line. The real obscenity is racism, sexism, poverty and class oppression.

June 1990

Chapter III

Economic Underdevelopment and the Contradictions of Capitalism

The Minimum Wage
and Poverty

Since George Bush became president nearly three months ago, one of the most hotly debated domestic policy issues to surface in Congress has been the controversy over the minimum wage. Since Reagan's election in 1980, the minimum wage mandated by the federal government has remained at the paltry sum of $3.35 per hour.

Hard-line conservatives are against any rise in the minimum wage, pointing out that the number of American workers who actually receive this wage has declined from nearly 8 million in 1981 to 3.9 million today. Moderate conservatives around Bush convinced him during last year's presidential campaign to embrace an increase in the minimum wage as a political foil to undermine Dukakis's popularity with low-income, white ethnic voters. After getting elected on a promise of "no new taxes," Bush wanted to back out of his commitment to a higher minimum wage. His lukewarm compromise was to hike the minimum wage to $3.65 next year, $3.95 in 1991, and $4.25 in 1992. However, there would also be a subminimum wage of $3.35 per hour for all new hires. This subminimum "training" wage would be required for six months, whether it's a first job or not.

The Bush proposal sparked a new tug of war between conservatives and liberals over the benefits vs. costs of a minimum wage. Reactionaries like former President Reagan insist that the minimum wage "has caused more misery and unemployment than anything since the Great Depression." They argue that whenever the minimum is raised, jobs are lost at the lowest pay levels. Small businesses which cannot afford to hike wages of semi-skilled or unskilled labor will lay off workers. The theory is that the market, not the government, should set wage rates. Consequently, the conservative National Federation of Independent Business has taken a posture to the right of Bush, claiming that there is "no need" to raise the minimum wage.

Liberal economists and politicians correctly point out that the current minimum wage is not sufficient for survival, and that it creates an economic barrier which unfairly hits blacks, hispanics and low income people the hardest. Statistically, roughly two-thirds of all workers who earn $3.35 an hour or less are women. Forty-two percent never completed high school, and only 4 percent are college graduates. Most are single, but those with families have an almost impossible challenge of feeding their families and paying rent on virtually no resources. Since 1981, the minimum wage has lost 39 percent due to inflation. A minimum wage rate of $4.60 per hour would be necessary just to keep pace with the 1981 rate.

A higher minimum wage would destroy some jobs, but by increasing the wages of nearly four million low-income workers, it would put more money into the economy through consumer spending. This in turn would create new jobs. Moreover, by lifting millions a small step away from poverty, a higher wage could reduce welfare rolls and government expenditures for social services.

The liberals' arguments are correct, but as always, they don't go far enough in analyzing the real problems confronting poor people. A higher minimum wage, even at $5.00 or $6.00 per hour, won't begin to address the crisis of poverty in America. In the eight years of the Reagan administration, low-income people—blacks, hispanics, Native Americans, Asians, and whites—experienced a devastating assault. Since 1981, more than one million people lost Aid to Families with Dependent Children benefits. Nearly one million people who would have been eligible for food stamps under the Carter Administration are now ineligible. Government subsidies for the construc-

tion of new low-income housing have been almost eliminated during the past six years. And the program which
provides an additional 13 weeks of unemployment benefits to jobless workers who have used up their basic 26
weeks of unemployment compensation has been almost
eliminated. In short, the economic "safety net" for the
working poor, those just above the government's poverty
line, has been ripped to shreds.

The minimum wage should be increased well above
$5.00 per hour, but that's only the beginning in addressing
the problem of systemic poverty and unemployment. A job
or guaranteed income for those who cannot work should
be considered a human right.

April 1989

Trends in the 1990s:
The Economic Crisis Ahead

The collapse of the Eastern European regimes and the democratic reforms occurring inside the Soviet Union have generated a kind of ideological euphoria within the ranks of American conservatives. Gorbachev, they argue, is the result of the $2 trillion military build-up under Ronald Reagan in the 1980s. The Russians are seeking peace because the American system of free enterprise and political democracy is superior. They point out that the Soviet economy is a mess, while the U.S. Gross National Product has reached $5.3 trillion by the end of the decade.

But this is an illusion of prosperity. The crisis which exists in the Soviet bloc is very real. Decades of political authoritarianism, inefficient, centralized planning, and the terror generated by secret police and violations of human rights contributed to the failure of the communist model. Yet the United States is not too far from its own economic crisis.

In the decade of the nineties, mounting political pressure will be targeted against the Pentagon's massive $300 billion annual budget. With the Soviets making serious reductions in armaments, the American military budget is not only wasteful but irrational. However, the Pentagon has a vested interest in maintaining an "external enemy," in order to justify spending billions of dollars for useless weaponry. Since the Soviets no longer fit the label "Evil Empire," American military planners will probably target three new potential "enemies"—China, Japan, and/or Germany. Japan's massive economic clout, plus the existence of a hard-line communist leadership in China, will be used to justify continued American military installations in the Far East. The specter of a united, militarized Germany, and threatening memories of World War II, could be used to promote a continued U.S. military presence in Europe.

The most overlooked victims of the Cold War have been the American people. For two generations, American politicians of both parties have lied about the so-called "Communist Menace" in order to suppress domestic progressive social protests, and to justify American imperialism abroad. But this kind of repression has a price—the billions of dollars taken away from domestic economic development and human needs. Today, the U.S. national debt comes to nearly $3 trillion, and the interest alone on this debt exceeds $160 billion annually.

Most of the new jobs generated in the 1980s were in the lowest paying, service sectors of the economy. More than one in eight Americans—and one out of three black Americans—live below the poverty level. The bottom one-fifth of all American families earn less than $8,900 annually. And two to three million Americans are now homeless, more than double the amount when Reagan was first elected president.

There are other signs that the Cold War and unchecked military spending contributed to the impending economic crisis within the United States. The Reagan and Bush administrations have had an economic philosophy of spend and borrow now, and worry about the future tomorrow. But the bill has come due. Recent estimates for the maintenance of all American highways for the next ten years exceed $300 billion. Just to repair all of the bridges in the United States would cost another $72 billion. To remove the hazardous wastes from toxic dumps comes to yet another $15 billion. Where's the money going to come from, when the majority of the white middle and upper classes are adamantly opposed to increased taxes for themselves?

Increasingly in the 1990s, American society will become more stratified by class and income. The upper classes, determined to maintain their own high standard of living, will look to the poor and working people to pay the costs for restructuring the collapsing economic system. Unfortunately, the Democratic Party will continue to move to the right, catering to the elite, and ignoring its black, Latino and working-class constituencies. This means that by the 1992 election, if there's an economic downturn, a major vacuum to the left of both major parties could exist. A real third party, based on the Rainbow Coalition's principles, could be the result.

January 1990

White America's Hidden Poor

The major weapon of America's corporate and political establishment used to divide working people is the idea of "race." Although we are a quarter-century removed from the racist rhetoric of George Wallace and Lester Maddox, racism continues to be a central factor which divides the electorate.

Many whites refuse to vote for black candidates over white challengers, even if they agree with their political philosophies and policies. Millions of white Democrats consistently vote for Republicans whenever their opponents are African Americans. In North Carolina's 1990 Senate race between liberal Democrat Harvey Gantt and controversial reactionary Jesse Helms, for instance, polls taken five days before the election placed Gantt with a 47 to 41 percent lead, with the rest undecided. On election day, Helms, the white Republican, won by a 52 to 48 percent margin. The entire shift in votes came from white Democrats and moderates who shared most of Gantt's views, but could not throw the lever for a black man.

Part of the problem lies in the perception that black politicians represent a "civil rights agenda," a set of so-called "special interests" advocating the rights of the poor, the unemployed, and those who experience the inequalities of discrimination, poor education, and inadequate health care. The civil rights agenda is projected by the white media establishment and by most Republicans as an agenda catering exclusively to blacks, having nothing in common with the conditions experienced by white people. Consequently, when black Democrats call for a national health care system to address the problems of infant mortality and preventable diseases such as hypertension, this is dismissed as a concession to minorities. When African-American leaders advocate expanded job training programs for high school dropouts, or increased federal expenditures for public housing projects and nutrition assistance to women, children and infants, conservatives denounce such efforts in a thinly veiled, racist discourse.

The suppression of all working people—white, Latino and African American—is the result. And the greatest tragedy of this technique of "divide and conquer" is that many white Americans themselves have little appreciation or awareness of the millions of poor whites who live in their own communities, and who share a basic economic kinship with oppressed people of color.

No one doubts that in a racist society, poverty and joblessness are allocated in a racist manner. A recent analysis of this country's 100 largest cities indicates that more than two-thirds of all residents of "extreme poverty neighborhoods"—that is, communities in which 40 percent or more of the population live below the poverty level—are black. Another 21 percent are Latino; only 10 percent are white. However, the fact remains that more than 60 percent of all Americans who live in poverty are white. Almost two-thirds of all Americans currently living in public housing projects are white. The overwhelming majority of American households receiving food stamps, or who benefit from public health programs for low-income people, are white.

White America's hidden poor can be found in the statistics of declining household earnings for working people since 1980. In the past 12 years, the average earnings of white household heads below age 25 have declined 19 percent. With the declining power of unions, and the explosion of semi-skilled and service industry jobs, the real income of millions of whites has fallen sharply.

More than ever, the black freedom movement must challenge the illusion that its agenda is "for blacks only." Jobs, social justice, and programs devoted to human needs are in the interests of the vast majority of all Americans, regardless of race.

April 1991

Black Self-Help, Entrepreneurship and Civil Rights

Several weeks ago, the University of Texas at Austin held its fifth annual Herman Sweatt Symposium on Civil Rights, on the topic of "Black Self-Help and Entrepreneurship." This symposium brought together a range of scholars and civic leaders, both conservative and liberal, to discuss the current problems and future of black economic development. The major speaker was Robert L. Woodson, president of the National Center for Neighborhood Enterprise, and a major conservative critic of the civil rights establishment.

Woodson and other conservative advocates of black enterprise tend to minimize the role of institutional racism as a barrier to African-American advancement, and place great faith in the ability of capitalism to resolve blacks' economic problems. Although Woodson and I clearly were at odds on politics, we found common ground in our mutual support for the values of excellence, individual initiative, and group economic mobilization. My own appreciation of the struggles of black small businesspeople comes from my own family's history.

For four generations, my father's family has produced a series of "entrepreneurs." My great-grandfather Morris Marable, a former slave, took 40 dollars in gold and two oxen as partial compensation for his many years of involuntary labor to his white master. With this "affirmative action" at the expense of his former owner, he was able to purchase some farmland, which grew into a productive cotton field. Saving carefully, he purchased a cotton gin, and for several decades was one of the few blacks who owned a business in his Black Belt community.

My grandfather, Manning Marable, was tutored in this independent, entrepreneurial spirit. Manning started a lumber mill during the Great Depression, and against the odds made a living for his wife and 13 children. His second oldest son and my father, James Marable, acquired a master's degree and became a school teacher. But dissatisfied with his family's economic situation, he took a second, night shift job for years, saving money to start his own nursery school for black children. Despite the lack of adequate sources of capital and credit, which were denied him solely on the basis of race, my father succeeded in establishing several enterprises. My father's seven brothers, based in Tuskegee, Alabama, started a series of construction companies and built several housing subdivisions and apartment complexes for African-American families.

What motivated my great-grandfather, grandfather, father and uncles was not just the satisfaction of making a profit. Their motivation was not simply in the creation of a product or service which people could use and enjoy. Generations of black entrepreneurs in my family were inspired by the goal of empowerment: controlling their own economic destinies, improving the quality of life and educational opportunities for their children despite institutional racism, the freedom from domination by whites, the satisfaction of making decisions and taking one's life into one's own hands. Empowerment is simultaneously economic, social, psychological and political, the quest to free oneself from the shackles of dependency to achieve greater independence.

Thousands of African Americans during the era of racial segregation established "mom and pop" enterprises, providing goods and services to the masses of blacks who were locked out of the larger white economy. Historically, black leaders across the ideological spectrum usually shared the goal of promoting economic self-sufficiency and capital formation within the black community. Nearly a century ago, conservative black educator Booker T. Washington established the National Negro Business League, an attempt to mobilize black-owned businesses. Washington's progressive critic, W.E.B. Du Bois, had come up with the concept of the League, and despite his socialist economic beliefs, always endorsed the concepts of black group economic development and black capital formation.

In the wake of the modern civil rights movement, the focus of black leadership shifted from desegregation, the dismantling of the legal apparatus of Jim Crow, to the integration of African Americans into the mainstream of government and society. Integrationist politics assumed that the decisive arena of black intervention would be within politics and government. By increasing the numbers of African Americans as mayors, Congresspeople and state legislators, blacks would be positioned to exercise greater power within society as a whole.

What this strategy failed to take into account was that legal segregation had created an artificial barrier which kept many white companies from establishing enterprises to cater to the black consumer market. The logic of integration increasingly forced black small businesses to compete against better-financed, larger firms, which could sell their goods and services at much lower prices.

Instead of funding an economic renaissance in the ghetto, integration essentially meant the draining of billions of dollars from black consumers into white companies. Secondly, the integrationist strategy relied heavily on the power of government to force open opportunities for private sector development. Even though the black private sector grew in size, reaching 339,000 black-owned firms by 1982, the economic viability of most enterprises was limited at best. The majority of black firms were concentrated in personal services and retail trade industries, and had average annual receipts of $5,000 or less, as of 1987. Black-owned businesses represented only 2 percent of all U.S. companies. Ironically, despite the achievement of voting rights, the actual economic conditions for millions of blacks were not advanced by the advocates of civil rights.

For decades, black elected officials have attempted to use their electoral influence to promote black-owned business development. The pioneer in this strategy was Maynard Jackson, first elected mayor of Atlanta in 1973, and also currently the city's mayor. Jackson was sensitive to the economic aspirations of black would-be entrepreneurs. His minority business enterprise (MBE) contracting program began to provide a way for blacks to obtain city contracts. In 1973, before Atlanta's MBE program was established, less than 0.1 percent, only $40,000, was allocated to minority-owned firms. Eight years later, almost one-fourth of Atlanta's city contracts went to black-owned companies, about $33 million.

Similarly, in Los Angeles, mayor Thomas Bradley also attempted to use the power of his office to promote African-American entrepreneurship. Prior to 1983, people of color and women consistently had received less than five percent of the city's contracts. By the late 1980s, Los Angeles's MBE program had increased that percentage for minorities and women to 16 percent of all construction, professional and technical services contracts. Los Angeles set aside $15 million to assist minority-owned firms to offer bids for the city's Metro-Rail projects, in order for them to obtain capital from local banks and to obtain the bonding required to compete for larger city contracts.

However, the problems of this entrepreneurial approach to black empowerment were many. First, most African-American elected officials and mayors were unwilling to challenge the deeply entrenched racism of their respective cities' corporate sectors. Most black-owned firms are concentrated in small retail and service sectors, mom-and-pop grocery stores and the like. White firms were much larger, had long histories of controlling city contracts, and had powerful friends inside the city's banking and legal establishment. Most white companies refused to form partnerships with minority-owned firms, and preferred to do business-as-usual. Consequently, there is little evidence which suggests that the election of an African-American mayor will lead to a fundamental restructuring of the business environment, promoting the creation of large numbers of strong black-owned businesses.

Second, there is at best mixed evidence indicating that a growing black enterprise sector can have a decisive or fundamental impact on creating jobs for many thousands of poor and lower-income blacks. The total number of blacks employed by black-owned firms is below one percent of the total black labor force in the United States. Most African-American firms are so small that they do not have a single paid employee. There is insufficient statistical evidence which shows that a typical black-owned business's profits are actually reinvested into black neighborhoods, black-owned banks or other institutions. Many affluent black entrepreneurs frequently live in white suburban neighborhoods; their profits are reinvested into white banks, securities and investments. So black entrepreneurship isn't benefiting the black community if it doesn't produce more investment capital and jobs for other African Americans.

Thirdly, changes in the federal government and courts threaten the entire strategy of using political leverage to consolidate black entrepreneurial gains. The Bush administration has given lip-service to supporting minority entrepreneurial development. The Minority Business Development Agency of the U.S. Commerce Department has been given a higher official profile. In 1989, President Bush created a Commission on Minority Business Development, chaired by Republican Joshua Smith, founder and CEO of the Maxima Corporation. This commission's final report is due this December. However, the Supreme Court's *Richmond v. Croson* decision, which undercut the use of minority set-asides, jeopardizes the whole effort by public officials to promote minority business development through public contracts.

Black conservatives like Robert Woodson, Clarence Thomas, Thomas Sowell, Walter Williams and others argue that black empowerment can occur through corporate capitalism, and an alliance with Reaganite Republicans. The fundamental weakness of their strategy lies in the simple fact that the actual material conditions separating people of color from the majority of white middle-to-upper-class people remain unequal. Fair competition in the marketplace is possible only when competitors have roughly equal access to capital and resources. The net wealth of an average white household today is $47,000; the net wealth of an average African-American household is barely $4,000. Blacks and hispanics still experience racial discrimination at banks when attempting to acquire business loans and mortgages. When the economic deck is stacked, the game is rigged. We need more black entrepreneurs and models of self-initiative, to be sure. But we must also demand that black businesspeople actually reinvest any profits back into the community. We must also have a fundamental reallocation of resources and change in the basic economic rules of the game, to maximize real opportunities for all.

May 1991

Black Workers in Crisis:
The Case of Flint, Michigan

Last month I spent several weeks lecturing in the Midwest and East Coast during African-American History Month. One of the most interesting and disturbing stops along the way was with the black community of Flint, Michigan. The social and economic devastation in Flint was largely created by the flight of General Motors from the town. The crisis which exists provides important lessons to African-American working people throughout the country.

Flint is rich in labor history. Back in 1937, during the Great Depression, thousands of black and white workers organized a massive sit-down strike against General Motors. The factories were occupied for 44 days, and hundreds of thugs were hired by management to destroy worker solidarity. Four thousand National Guardsmen, equipped with machine guns, bayonets and tear gas, were ordered to crush the strike. At the last minute, negotiators reached a compromise settlement greatly beneficial to the workers.

What has happened since this landmark sit-down strike? The people of Flint were told that they could trust the good intentions of General Motors. GM and the auto industry in general were committed to protecting the interests of working people. But in the 1970s, GM began taking the profits produced by working people and exporting them in the form of new plants outside of the United States. By the middle of the 1980s nearly one-third of the parts in the typical GM car were produced outside of the United States. The same kinds of trends also occurred in other industries. The big auto companies claimed that they were hemorrhaging millions a day, and that working people had to make economic concessions in order to keep their jobs.

The city government of Flint made major concessions. Between 1976 and 1986, the Flint city council gave GM a 50 percent cut in taxes on $1.3 billion worth of property. GM promised it would use the tax abatement to make new jobs, and to save existing jobs. Instead, GM eliminated 18,000 jobs.

GM began to take Michigan cities and townships to court in the 1980s, demanding dramatic reductions in property taxes. Saginaw's city officials agreed to give GM a 31 percent tax reduction.

Despite workers' concessions, the economic destruction continued. Thousands continued to be laid off. In December 1986, GM closed the Flint Chevy V-6 engine plant. In May 1987, it closed the Flint Truck and Bus Line. Nationally, about a quarter-million GM workers lost their jobs in the 1970s through the mid-1980s. In the 1980s, more than 30,000 people left Flint to look for employment opportunities.

The changes in the auto industry have had a disproportionately negative impact on the African-American community. There are several ways to measure this impact. Changes in technology, and the use of cybernation, have eliminated thousands of jobs. According to one study by Samuel D.K. James, in 1985 about 40 percent of the white workers who had lost their jobs between 1979 and 1984 had not found replacement employment; during the same period, the figure for displaced black workers was 60 percent. In a short three-year period, from 1977-1980, there was a decline of almost 50,000 black auto workers at Ford, Chrysler and GM, who were largely replaced by technological changes in the work process.

Blacks comprise only about 11 percent of the U.S. workforce, but they still account for 17 percent of the labor force for GM, Chrysler and Ford. Black auto workers earned over $3 billion in wages last year. However, between 1979 and 1984, manufacturing employment for all U.S. industries declined by 18 percent, while manufacturing jobs held by blacks declined 27 percent.

In the states where automobile production is dominant—the Great Lakes region—black manufacturing employment fell 36 percent. Many of the new Japanese auto factories are being located in areas where there are significantly lower populations of blacks than older auto-producing areas.

Today, sections of Flint look like they've been blasted with neutron bombs. Black youth unemployment is over 50 percent. Teenagers complain that they have only four real options: working at minimum wage; becoming pregnant and existing on welfare; joining the armed services; or selling drugs. The economic crisis has generated black-on-black crime, alcoholism, drug abuse and the disruption of many institutions such as the black church.

The solution to the crisis of black working-class people isn't more concessions. We need legislation restricting the powerful corporations from moving capital and factories outside the United States, and from state to state. More importantly, we need new, aggressive leadership in organized labor to fight for workers' interests. We need to revive the militancy of the 1937 sit-down strike, demanding that a job, health care, and a drug-free community are human rights.

March 1990

Racism and Corporate America

For years, Reagan economist Milton Friedman asserted that the free enterprise system is virtually "free" of racism. More recently, black Reaganites such as Thomas Sowell and Walter Williams have championed the corporations as being interested in the uplifting and development of African Americans. But the actual record of the relationship between blacks and corporate America, particularly in terms of black employment in managerial positions, has been similar to *apartheid* in South Africa.

Before 1965, the white corporate establishment didn't realize that African Americans even existed. College-trained blacks and middle-class businesspeople were attached to the separate economy of the ghetto. African Americans who applied for jobs at white-owned companies found that their resumes weren't accepted. Blacks who were hired were placed in low-paying clerical or maintenance positions.

With the impact of the civil rights movement, the public demonstrations and boycotts against corporations which Jim Crowed blacks, businesses were forced to change their hiring policies. However, most blacks were placed in minority neighborhoods, having little contact with whites in supervisory roles. In the 1960s and 1970s, the careers of most black executives were "racialized." They were given responsibilities which focused exclusively on racial matters, rather than the broad issues which affected the profit and loss of the corporation as a whole. They were assigned to mediate black employees' grievances, or to direct affirmative action policies, rather than being placed in charge of a major division of the company. Their managerial experiences were limited, and therefore their prospects for upward mobility into senior executive positions were nonexistent.

In 1977, only 3.6 percent of all managers in the United States were people of color. The *Fortune* magazine survey of the 1,000 largest U.S. companies that year indicated that, out of 1,708 senior executives, there were only three African Americans, two Asians, two hispanics, and eight women.

In the 1980s and 1990s, progress for African Americans inside corporations slowed, and in some cases has been reversed. African Americans now represent about 13 percent of the total U.S. population, but less than 5 percent of all managers, and less than 1 percent of all mid-to-upper level executives. Why this pattern of corporate apartheid?

One reason is the racial segregation of U.S. business schools. African Americans represent only 3 to 4 percent of all students in MBA programs. Blacks are less than 2 percent in graduate level programs in the sciences and computer programming. With the Bush administration's threat to eliminate minority scholarships at universities, and a decline in federal enforcement of affirmative action, universities aren't as aggressive in recruiting students of color.

Many heads of major corporations have racial attitudes which are discriminatory. But even more pervasive is what I would term the "passive racism" inside the corporate suites. White executives recognize that racism exists within their corporations, but they are unwilling to do anything about it. They refuse to compensate victims of past or current discrimination, or to take positive steps to subsidize development programs within minority communities, such as internships or scholarships.

Black and hispanic executives usually lack the informal connections most whites take for granted. They usually don't belong to the same social clubs, churches, fraternities or political parties. They aren't mentored for possible openings for career advancement by senior white executives. From their perspective, a "glass ceiling" exists which blocks their mobility.

Unless policies of greater corporate accountability and social responsibility are pursued, blacks, Latinos and women will continue to be marginalized inside corporations. Part of this strategy for reform must transcend the request for jobs within the corporate structure. The private sector must be forced to address the basic needs of the black community. This will not occur until the system of corporate capitalism is transformed, and economic decisions are based first upon human needs rather than private profits.

March 1991

Chapter IV

In Pursuit
of Educational Equality

The Black Male
and Higher Education

The avenue of higher education, which was the pathway toward socioeconomic advancement for several generations of blacks, appears to be coming to a dead end. According to the *Chronicle of Higher Education*, black Americans earned 820 research doctorates in 1986, less than 75 percent of the number they received 10 years before. The decline was concentrated solely among black males. Black men earned only 321 research doctorates in 1986, compared to 684 doctorates in 1977. By comparison, the number of doctorates received by black women was 499—more than 15 percent higher than in 1977.

These recent statistics conform with the general impression of most observers that black males are rapidly disappearing from the arena of higher education, across the board. First, there's been a sharp decline in the number of black males who are graduating from high school and enrolling directly into colleges and universities. In 1976, 34 percent of all black high school graduates enrolled in college; by 1985, that figure had declined to 26 percent. Virtually the entire decline had been directly the result of lower enrollment of males. For instance, from 1980 to 1984, the total number of black women in college declined only slightly, from 539,857 to 529,096. But the figure for black males declined by 25,300, down to 368,089. The current ratio of black males to females in the nation's college classrooms is 30 males to every 70 females. An unequal gender ratio is apparent at virtually every coeducational college where blacks are present. At Hampton University, for instance, 2,900 black women were enrolled as of last autumn, compared to 1,618 black men. At Georgia State University, there are 2,450 black women students and only 1,215 black men.

Once they're enrolled, moreover, black males tend to receive the worst grades, and have far more difficulties making the adjustment to college life. They have more difficulty with language and writing skills than most black females. Consequently, fewer black men are graduating and entering professional careers with bachelor's degrees. According to the *Chronicle of Higher Education,* black men earned 25,634 B.A. degrees in 1976, and only 23,018 B.A.'s in 1984, a more than 10 percent decline. During the same years, the number of B.A. degrees achieved by black women increased by 2.9 percent, from 33,488 to 34,455.

Why are black males disappearing from colleges? Part of the answer resides in the cultural attack against the image of the successful black male. Negative stereotypes which project most black men as pimps, drug addicts, criminals and the unemployed are readily found in movies, magazines and books. Black young males frequently grow to maturity without sufficient male role models who project images of confidence and security. Teachers, principals and other authority figures often expect young black men to fail, and their unsteady performance in the classroom becomes a self-fulfilling prophesy. Instead of steering young black males into math, computer science and other college preparatory courses, they are usually channelled into vocational education.

Black male unemployment rates are more than twice that for white males, so there is always pressure placed upon young black men to quit school and to find jobs in order to support their families. The army becomes the "employer of last resort" for many desperate black men. Not surprisingly, the number of black men serving in the armed forces increased from 288,623 in 1976 to 356,583 in 1987. Similarly, thousands more between the ages of 18 and 35 are disproportionately located in public mental hospitals, prisons and jails. Those who question the connections between poverty, poor education and imprisonment need to consider this: over 50 percent of all black males who are arrested are unemployed at the time of their incarceration, and the majority of all black prisoners have less than an eleventh grade education.

What are the long-term consequences of the disappearing black male from college campuses? The decline of Afro-American males in higher education will help to accelerate social class and income stratification within the black community. For instance, black college graduates' real incomes, adjusted for inflation, jumped 6.5 percent between 1973 and 1986. During the same 13-year period, black high school graduates lost 44 percent of their real earning power. Young black males with college degrees have unemployment rates of six to eight percent; young black males who drop out of high school have jobless rates of 33 percent and above. Sociologist William Julius Wilson correctly notes: "As fewer black men go to college, there will be fewer of them in professional and managerial positions, and more in blue-collar occupations."

February 1988

False Prophet: Joe Clark

Joe Clark, the crusading black principal of Eastside High School, Patterson, New Jersey, has received a great amount of media attention and public praise in recent weeks. And when viewed superficially, it's easy to praise Clark as a valiant educator who's been unjustly maligned by liberals of various stripes.

Clark was named principal of one of New Jersey's worst public schools about six years ago. Eastside was overrun by drugs and violence, and Clark was determined to turn things around. Cultivating a style which was simultaneously provocative, confrontational and charismatic, he patrolled school corridors with a bullhorn, shouting out orders. Clark promoted the Protestant work ethic, and praised young women who were virgins for upholding morality. The principal criticized families who relied upon welfare as lazy, and condemned difficult students as "leeches, miscreants and hoodlums." Although the principal had no legal authority to expel students without the approval of the Patterson School Board, Clark purged 300 of Eastside's 3,000 students in 1982, and in late 1987 he banned an additional 60 students.

Clark's preemptive actions stirred a hornet's nest of public criticism. Educators condemned Clark's actions as counterproductive, noting that under New Jersey law, all individuals are entitled to a public education until age 21. Patterson's School Board condemned Clark, and ordered him to reinstate the 60 pupils who had recently been expelled. But a groundswell of support for Clark occurred, initially from many working-class and poor black residents of Patterson who favored a hard-line approach on educational issues. Supporters noted that scores on the Scholastic Aptitude Test for Eastside students had risen since Clark's tenure, as well as school marks on the statewide proficiency test for math and English composition.

Since January, Clark has become something of an instant celebrity in the media. He was featured on ABC's *Nightline;* rap musicians Run-DMC consented to perform a concert at Eastside High School to salute Clark. Secretary of Education William Bennett applauded Clark as a "national folk hero. He rescued a school that was going down the drain and made it into a school that was functioning," Bennett proclaimed. The black principal has emphasized his intellectual kinship to the Reaganites, and currently displays a large, framed portrait of Ronald Reagan in his office. Clark states that the welfare system, affirmative action policies, and the social agendas of "hocus pocus liberals" are largely to blame for the black community's ills. Without his firm control and unyielding policies toward social deviants, Clark insists, the school would quickly fall backward into disgrace. "When I leave this school," he brags, "if it didn't plummet to the depths of despair, if it didn't become violence-ridden, if drugs and stabbings...did not reappear, I would be chagrined."

But how effective has Clark really been? The slight rise in aptitude scores can be explained partially from the fact that many low-achieving students are purged from school rolls, thus artificially elevating overall scores. And even the test score increases are marginal at best. At Eastside, less than half of all students pass math and writing proficiency tests, while statewide averages were 77 percent and 86 percent, respectively. Substantial evidence indicates that Clark brutally harasses and intimidates faculty and students alike. Clark called one teacher "half a black man" in front of other colleagues, and described one dissident group of teachers as "gutless, spineless, racist bastards." According to the Patterson Education Association, many good teachers have resigned or transferred from Eastside "under duress."

Clark presents himself as a tough-minded educator, an urban prophet struggling for quality standards in the public schools. Regrettably, some blacks have cheered his bombastic and bullying tactics, thinking that bullhorns and expulsions are a substitute for real education. But Clark is a false prophet, a shallow and demagogic administrator who prefers to exert authority at the expense of the broader goal of enriching the educational experience for inner-city black and hispanic youth. The Reaganites see in Clark a cheap but sensational way to win over a fragment of the ghetto's black working class, frustrated by poor schools and high crime rates. But Clark's strategy is nothing but a dead end.

February 1988

The Politics
of Black Student Activism

Twenty years ago, in the wake of Dr. Martin Luther King's assassination, thousands of outraged black students protested white racism on their college campuses. They established new militant organizations called Black Student Unions, or BSUs. I was more than an observer in this political process. At Earlham College in Indiana, I was the chairperson of our BSU in 1969. As we explore the factors behind racism at white colleges today, we should also examine the changing role and function of BSUs.

As originally conceived, the BSUs wanted to create a greater social and political awareness among African-American students, and a desire to confront and to challenge white administrators on matters of educational policy. They called for the creation of the Black Studies departments, Minority Student Programs, Cultural Centers, and other institutions. The BSUs advanced the cause of affirmative action by demanding the recruitment and appointment of black faculty and administrators. The BSUs represented a vital link between the struggles being waged in urban streets and our communities with the politics of higher education which existed at white academic institutions.

The politicized character of the BSUs always depended upon two basic factors: the relative strength or weakness of the national and local black protest movement at any given time, and the specific type of black students being recruited by particular colleges in any year. As the struggle markedly declined in the mid-to-late 1970s, it became increasingly difficult to interest many black students to be personally involved in protests, demonstrations or even community-oriented programs. Many colleges also ceased recruiting black and hispanic students from low-income neighborhoods and inner-city areas, and deliberately focused their efforts on minority youth at private high schools or mid-to-upper income school districts. The Reagan administration reinforced this strategic shift in student recruitment by drastically cutting student loan and aid programs, which meant that low-income black families could no longer afford to accumulate modest amounts of money to send their sons and daughters to college. It should not be surprising, therefore, that many BSUs became more conservative in the 1980s. On some campuses, the BSU became the functional equivalent of a sorority or fraternity. They became heavily involved in social activities, and disengaged from political and academic institutions. At many schools, the BSU disappeared entirely, its records and archives lost forever. And at other institutions, there was a renaissance of black fraternities and sororities as the central agencies of student interest and collective activity.

In this environment of political retrenchment and reaction, in the twilight of the civil rights era, it was difficult for many Black Studies departments and programs to survive, much less develop and expand. Within BSUs, interest in maintaining student involvement and support for all black academic programs declined.

In order to reverse the trend toward institutional racism in white higher education, blacks must recognize the connection between political struggle, institution-building and educational change. Without strong black student organizations, there is no viable constituency which can reinforce black educators. Without strong and assertive black academic and student supportive service institutions on white campuses, affirmative action programs are meaningless. It makes little sense to recruit black students into white universities, only to see them drop out within months because of the absence of strong, supportive institutions on campus. Educational progress for black youth fundamentally depends upon a political and academic awareness and self-organization.

March 1988

Black Colleges
and White Academic Racism

This autumn, enrollment at many historically black colleges and universities increased dramatically. This was particularly true for poor colleges which had experienced severe economic turmoil only a few years ago. For instance, my wife's undergraduate alma mater, Knoxville College of Tennessee, increased its enrollment to 1,301 students, a jump of 100 percent in only one year.

At nearby Fisk University in Nashville, enrollment surged 19 percent to 744 students. Florida A&M University's freshman class was 15 percent larger than last year's. South Carolina State's enrollment increased by 9 percent; student enrollment at Jackson State University jumped 12 percent; Alabama State University's student body increased by 14 percent. At Norfolk State University, total enrollment has reach an "all-time high of more than 8,000 students," according to the *Chronicle of Higher Education*.

Why the renaissance of interest in historically black colleges? All observers would agree that it's too soon to predict with any degree of confidence that all these black colleges have turned the fiscal corner toward stability and growth. Sheer numbers of students do not make an institution economically viable. There's an immediate need to expand the endowments for all black colleges, in order to sustain recent growth. Larger numbers of students also place a severe strain on existing resources, because these schools must hire more professors and staff, and spend more on physical facilities. Unless resources and personnel keep pace with student enrollment, the actual quality of education can decline.

There are several reasons for the increase in black college enrollments. First, there's the economics of college tuition. The average black family's household income is below $20,000 annually. Only a small minority of black families have the economic resources to cover college costs at most white institutions. For example, since 1978, the average annual price of four-year public colleges for tuition and fees rose from $651 to $1,566. At private institutions, tuition and fees have risen during the same years from $2,647 to $7,693. This year, tuition and fees at major institutions have skyrocketed: for out-of-state students, it costs $11,990 to attend Georgetown University; $12,250 at New York University; $13,285 at the University of Chicago; and $13,380 at Princeton. By contrast, Morris Brown College's tuition and fees for 1988-89 were $4,840; Tougaloo College, $3,756; and LeMoyne-Owen College, $3,380.

A more serious factor must be the disturbing escalation of racist violence and harassment of black students at white institutions. No one spends thousands of dollars for a child's education only to have one's son or daughter subjected to racist abuse. Although a number of white universities initiated this academic year with workshops and lectures on racial sensitivity and cultural tolerance, many others have done nothing to reeducate their white students. In the racist climate produced in part by the policies of the Reagan administration, many white college students have internalized the message that the civil rights movement is over, affirmative action is dead, and any specific grievances raised by black students or the civil rights movement in general can be ignored.

Not surprisingly, a political culture of racial reaction breeds racist violence. At the University of Wisconsin-Madison, a white fraternity organized a "slave auction," which included vulgar racist slurs. White students at DePauw University, Indiana, sponsored a "ghetto party," complete with racist stereotypes. There have been at least

150 "racial incidents" on white college campuses during the past two years. The Justice Department has also investigated over 300 incidents of racist confrontations and violence during 1987. As our society moves sharply towards greater racial inequality and class divisions, black colleges become one of the few hopes for educational opportunity for minorities. As the white educational establishment turns its back to racial tolerance and pluralism, blacks are forced to return to options of the pre-Jim Crow segregation era.

November 1988

The Crisis in Western Culture

A central crisis which characterizes the white western world today, especially its educational institutions, is a cultural crisis.

For centuries, white America and Western European educational institutions have established their curricula and educational assumptions upon a series of ethnocentric distortions. Creative, talented black intellectuals, writers, poets and scientists are traditionally ignored, while the architects of slavery, racism and economic oppression are championed. For example, Aristotle, the father of modern western philosophy, was also the earliest defender of slavery and the "natural" inferiority of slaves and women. Do the writings of Protestant reformer Martin Luther provide the sole treatment of religion worthy of study—or should we also turn to the thoughts of Martin Luther King, Jr.? Does Thomas More's Utopia or the Leviathan of Thomas Hobbes tell us more about politics than the writings of Frantz Fanon or C.L.R. James? Can a young black woman or man learn better about life by reading a white novelist, or by reading Toni Morrison, Alice Walker or Richard Wright? Which is more relevant to an understanding of humanity, Plato or W.E.B. Du Bois?

When education reflects the mythology that the white West has created for itself, the answers to these questions become obvious. The curriculum in traditionally white, mainstream environments reinforces ethnocentrism and an ignorance of the cultural and intellectual creativity of nonwhites.

Black and progressive educators have long recognized that the cultural battleground is absolutely decisive in the broader political and economic empowerment of oppressed people. The values which are taught to our children largely determine their behavior. If a people are not seen as active creators of culture, playing a significant role in history, they will be ignored within our children's textbooks and classes.

In America, our economic system rewards people who possess certain values and styles of behavior, such as aggressiveness, competitiveness, initiative and individualism. But in their most extreme form, reinforced by the constant quest for dollars, such values in people deteriorate into greed and materialism. Culture becomes anything which can be marketed for a profit. The media reflects the lowest level of public awareness and political discussion—"trash TV," symbolized by Geraldo Rivera, is the logical result. Sexuality all too often becomes simply a commodity, an item which can be bought and sold. Religion becomes marketed by hypocritical televangelists seeking dollars and wealth more than the salvation of souls.

The cultural conflict is waged most intensely in the field of education, and especially on college campuses. White, conservative traditionalists are fighting against any changes in the Western civilization courses, to ensure that the next generation of white young people is properly indoctrinated in reactionary, racist values. At Stanford University, after two years of bitter debate, the faculty senate voted to overthrow the university's Western Civilization course requirement. The new required course includes readings by people of color. Stanford's modest acknowledgement of nonwhite cultures within its curriculum has been denounced by former Education Secretary William J. Bennett, who condemned the university for "trashing the classics" and capitulating to students' demands.

As America becomes increasingly black, hispanic and Asian in its population, academic institutions will be pressured to change their curricula to reflect the cultural values and literatures of nonwhites. The phasing out of the western culture program foreshadows a more intense future struggle over faculty and administrative posts, and the entire curriculum as well. As students begin to read Du Bois, Baldwin, Hurston, Robeson and others, they inevitably acquire a critical perspective on racial issues, which assumes a linkage between scholarship and social reform. Art, music, and literature for Afro-Americans is also a critique of injustice and racism.

January 1989

The Educational "Underclass"

In the 1980s, sociologists have popularized a new term which describes the permanent poverty of millions of poorly-trained and uneducated residents of the urban ghetto—the "underclass." This terminology suggests that millions of poor people, mostly blacks and Latinos, are so thoroughly marginalized by the lack of jobs, decent schools, health care and other institutions that they become virtually irrelevant to the process of production. Many exist at minimum wages or less, or via semi-legal or extralegal means, such as hustling, drugs and petty crime. I have a number of reservations about the term "underclass," in part because it tends to underestimate the centrality and utility of racism in perpetuating impoverished conditions for people of color.

But if an economic "underclass" does exist, its perpetuation and expansion are largely guaranteed by the tragic situation in our public schools. At a time when our economy is demanding a higher level of technical ability, mathematic and scientific skills for the labor force, fewer young people are being academically prepared. The *Wall Street Journal* recently documented a series of disturbing facts about the educational underclass.

In many states, the dropout rate for nonwhite high school students exceeds 50 percent. Across the United States, 3,800 teenagers drop out of school *every day*. And of those students who stay in schools, millions don't receive any serious training in algebra, geometry, biology, English composition, history or foreign languages.

Approximately 80 percent of all applicants interviewed by Motorola, Inc., fail an entry-level examination which requires seventh grade English and fifth-grade math. According to the *Journal*, in 1988 New York Telephone Company received 117,000 applications for only several hundred full-time jobs. Less than half of the applicants were considered qualified to take the basic employment exam, and of this number only 2,100 passed. In short, thousands of people are applying for jobs as cashiers and bank tellers who cannot do simple arithmetic. Thousands of high school students are unable to read the simplest instructions. Meanwhile, the new jobs generated by high technology increasingly demand the ability to operate computers and to analyze complex data. The gap is steadily growing between the technical qualifications and academic background necessary for such jobs, and the actual level of ability of millions in the educational underclass.

Part of the solution would appear to be the recruitment and retention of highly motivated and excellent teachers in the public school systems, especially in the sciences and mathematics. In recent years, there's been a renewed interest in becoming public school teachers among college students. Back in 1982, only 4.7 percent of all college freshman polled wanted to be teachers; by 1988, the percentage jumped to 8.8 percent. But the bulk of these students aren't science majors. Only 1,500 education majors qualify to teach high school math or science each year, or about one for every ten jobs which are advertised in these fields. In the next five years, about 625,000 young men and women will be trained in colleges to become school teachers—but in that period, there will be a need for more than one million new teachers. One-fourth of all public school instructors will retire in the next 15 years, and a high percentage of younger teachers who are discouraged by low pay and poor working conditions will quit.

It won't be long before a new form of "segregation" will exist to threaten the prospects of millions of black youth. There won't be the Jim Crow signs of "white" and "colored" to preserve job discrimination. Instead, the new segregation of the twenty-first century could be the division between the educated "haves" and the uneducated "have nots." Those who lack scientific, mathematical and computer skills are already disproportionately nonwhite. The struggle for expanded federal expenditures for student grants and improved public schools is directly linked to the economic future of black America.

May 1989

Beyond Academic Apartheid

Although Ronald Reagan is no longer in the White House, the reactionary racial sentiment he inspired and encouraged continues to fester into ugly violence. This is particularly true on college campuses across the country. At Brown University in Rhode Island, for example, racist epithets and posters began to be circulated in dormitories last spring. This fall, a number of African American and Asian students have been verbally assaulted by gangs of whites yelling from automobiles. In the past eight weeks, there have also been at least 16 reported cases of blacks robbing or assaulting whites on campus and in the city. Brown president Vartan Gregorian announced in response to the crisis that he was considering requesting federal assistance "to prosecute the perpetrators of such cowardly acts."

Although black students and faculty deplored these assaults against whites, it also appeared that these incidents could be used to polarize racial relations still further. White students sharply criticized Gregorian for condemning only racist attacks by whites, and for doing too little to protect whites' security and personal property. Dean of Students John Robinson declared that "black students should not be upset if campus police ask them for identification." Brown Vice President Robert Reichley subsequently attempted to clarify Robinson's controversial statement, declaring that only "suspicious people will be checked." For many students of color, there was a sense that only they would be classified as "suspicious," and that the institution was unable to take decisive measures to create a truly culturally pluralistic and safe environment.

At Michigan State University last May, over 400 students held a sit-in at the main administration building to challenge institutional racism. Students called for more aggressive recruitment of minority faculty, additional scholarship funds for nonwhites, and the creation of a new position of minority advisor to the provost. Student leaders now say that progress at Michigan State remains too slow, and that more unrest is possible. And at Tulane University in New Orleans last month, a Ku Klux Klan-style cross was burned in front of a white fraternity house which had just offered membership to an African-American student.

These incidents, plus dozens more, illustrate that despite all of the reforms within higher education, racism is still alive and well. Despite the introduction of Black Studies and ethnic studies courses, minority student services groups, and affirmative action policies, "academic apartheid" has actually intensified. The essential dilemma is quite simple. Well-meaning white college administrators have perceived the issue of racism as a "black problem," or a dilemma of "minority adjustment" and mobility within the academic "mainstream." Actually, racism is not a "black problem," but a problem generated by the economic, political and social consequences of white power and privilege. People of color should not be asked to "adjust" to the white environment of the university; the white university itself must accommodate to our needs and interests. The curriculum, personnel hiring policies and administrative structure must meet the legitimate concerns of all people of color, if the system and rhetoric of academic apartheid is to be transcended.

What practical steps are required to create an environment of multiculturalism and diversity within academic institutions? The first and most crucial step is the articulation of a coherent philosophy of cultural diversity, which is endorsed by a college's president, provost and board of trustees. There's a need for leadership, vision and commitment at the top. If a college president is personally apathetic about racist harassment of students, or doesn't personally care if faculty job searches yield no nonwhite applicants, this attitude is directly communicated to lower-level administrators, department chairs and faculty. As former presidential candidate Michael Dukakis correctly observed about the Reagan administration's corruption: "The fish stinks from the head down." Similarly, a pluralistic academic environment and a sense of community are largely set by the attitudes and personal commitments of the academic leadership.

The university must take direct steps to punish racist behavior and rhetoric. You don't take aspirin to recover from cancer, and you shouldn't take half-measures in addressing and uprooting racism. The college administration must make it clear and unambiguous to all students that it will not condone or tolerate any acts or language which would be generally interpreted as racist. Students must understand that there is a basic distinction between exercising their freedom of speech and the use of racist speech which terrorizes and intimidates people of color, destroying the sense of community. Students who are found guilty of using racist speech, or committing acts of violence against people of color, must be disciplined severely. Faculty who may be guilty of employing racist rhetoric in the classroom, or who have grading policies which are designed to discriminate against African Americans and other people of color, should be removed from teaching in the classroom.

Affirmative action policies must also be aggressive and innovative. It isn't sufficient to create an affirmative action office which has the authority to monitor the employment searches for new faculty and staff. Affirmative action begins with the definition of departmental and institutional needs and priorities. A history department which has no black faculty and also has no one teaching African-American and African history must be challenged to define its next available job search in these disciplines. An English department which lacks scholars/teachers in African-American, Caribbean or African literature seriously handicaps all students intellectually. By defining a new faculty appointment in these areas, a department can increase the probability of recruiting a candidate who is also an African-American scholar.

Affirmative action should mean that administrators must use their authority to block faculty appointment if, in their judgement, a department's search committee did not take extensive steps to identify and attempt to recruit minority candidates. And affirmative action offices must be funded to support research and teaching activities which will create a more racially diverse academic environment on campuses. These steps, as well as many others, can create a more democratic and non-racist education.

November 1989

In Pursuit
of Educational Equality

Nearly 40 years ago, in late 1952, the Supreme Court heard the historic case, *Brown v. Board of Education of Topeka,* which would outlaw racial segregation in public schools. *Brown* was the culmination of 20 years' legal strategy by the NAACP's legal staff, directed by Charles Hamilton Houston and Thurgood Marshall. The High Court's decision declared unanimously that "in the field of public education the doctrine of 'separate but equal' has no place. Separate educational facilities are inherently unequal." The *Brown* decision led directly to the important Montgomery bus boycott movement which catapulted Martin Luther King, Jr. into political prominence, and eventually shattered the system of Jim Crow.

More than a generation has passed since the great victories of the civil rights movement. Our cities have become more racially segregated than ever before; public schools in urban areas have deteriorated with declining tax bases and the flight of the middle classes to the suburbs. The signs reading "white" and "colored" are no longer present in the doorways of our schools, but the segregation of income, poverty and the ghetto has, in effect, reversed the *Brown* decision. Millions of black, Latino and low-income children are being deprived of a quality education, because school systems are unable to provide the academic tools necessary for learning.

Last month, the Supreme Court took another decisive step away from the legacy of *Brown.* In a 5-3 ruling in an Oklahoma City case, the Court made it easier for cities to halt school busing for desegregation, even when their schools remain rigidly polarized by race. The Court's majority declared that a locality could terminate a desegregation order in its school system if it eliminated the "vestiges of past discrimination...to the extent practicable" in hiring policies, students' school assignments, transportation, and facilities. A school system had to show that it made efforts to comply with desegregation orders within a vaguely termed "reasonable period of time." Chief Justice William Rehnquist, speaking for the majority, stated that "Federal supervision of local school systems was intended as a temporary measure to remedy past discrimination." Rehnquist's ruling utterly failed to take into account that institutional racism did not disappear with the end of Jim Crow segregation. In dissent, Associate Justice Thurgood Marshall wrote: "The majority suggests that 13 years of desegregation (in Oklahoma City schools) was enough. I strongly disagree."

More than 400 school districts across the country are under a court-ordered desegregation plan, including Cleveland, Dallas, Chicago, Buffalo, and Phoenix. Many of these school boards will use this decision to void the impact of *Brown,* accelerating educational inequality.

The way forward beyond the current impasses created by the Rehnquist Court may be provided in a recent legal suit filed, on behalf of 37 children, in state circuit court in Montgomery, Alabama, against the Alabama Department of Education and other agencies supervising public schools. The suit challenges the amount of money allocated per student in Alabama's 129 school districts. Litigants pointed out that schools in one white district receive $4,302 per student, compared to only $2,563 per child in a poor, predominantly black school district. Nearly two-thirds of all local school district financing comes from the state government, and only one-sixth comes from property taxes.

The suit charges that the state of Alabama's formula for allocating educational funds is inherently discriminatory, and should be declared unconstitutional. Alabama is the fourteenth state in the past four years to be sued over the issue of school financing.

It is clear that the majority of white Americans no longer support busing for school integration. In order to improve urban schools for minority children, our most effective means is the unequal allocation of financial resources between districts, to upgrade the quality of schooling in low-income areas. This is the next challenge in the struggle for educational equality.

February 1991

Chapter V

Racism and Apartheid: Along the Color Line

The Two Faces of Racism

Much has been written about the tragic, racially-motivated execution of 16-year-old Yusuf K. Hawkins in the Bensonhurst neighborhood of Brooklyn. When Hawkins and several black friends visited the white neighborhood on 23 August to look at a used car, they were attacked by approximately ten white youths. Reportedly, the white youths were outraged that a local white woman was dating a black man, and they were lying in wait for their victim. Armed with baseball bats, golf clubs and at least one gun, they were heard by witnesses saying before the shooting: "Let's club the nigger." Young Hawkins backed away from the confrontation, but was gunned down by two .32 caliber bullets.

Hawkins's murder triggered a deep outrage among the city's African-American population for several reasons. Hawkins was only the latest of a series of black victims of white violence in New York, a list which has included the black men beaten and killed at Howard Beach, and the killing of Michael Stewart, Eleanor Bumpers and other blacks by the police. When local activists Jitu Weusi, Reverend Herbert Daughtry and others called for a protest march to denounce the murder, they were told by New York Mayor Ed Koch that they had no right to protest in the Bensonhurst area. On August 31, thousands participated in a mile-long protest march, which culminated in a confrontation with police on the Brooklyn Bridge. About ten police and scores of demonstrators were injured. On the same day, the suspected killer of Hawkins, Joseph Fama, pleaded not guilty to the crime.

The deeper reason for the level of anger among black residents was the viciousness of the murder, and its random character. Hawkins was not engaging in any criminal activity. He was only inquiring about an automobile for sale. The fact that he could be killed in cold blood told the city's 2.2 million African Americans that they, too, could become victims of vigilante violence by white racists at any moment. As in South Africa, blacks had to fear for their personal safety if they walked through certain all-white districts.

A typical reaction was that of Devin S. Standard, a black executive, in the *New York Times*. Despite Standard's education, white business associates, white girlfriend and Republican Party affiliations, "I am intrigued by the fact that apparently there are gangs of white people just waiting to kill me. What have I done?" Standard asked for an entire generation of young black men. "What have we African-Americans done that makes so many white people hate, fear and disdain us so much that they want to deprive us of our lives, liberty and pursuit of happiness? Do white people aspire to intern us all?"

Standard and millions of black Americans under 25 years of age have no personal memories of Jim Crow segregation, and were too young to participate in the Black Power movement. They have grown up in the era of Reaganism and the decline of the civil rights movement. Overt discrimination has given way to more subtle forms of racism. Because younger African Americans believed the illusion of American democracy and equality for people of color, they were shocked and stunned by Hawkins's murder. They can't comprehend that Klan-style violence still exists today.

Vigilante violence, police brutality and other forms of brutality are the most obvious face of American racism. But far more pervasive and influential is the second face of discrimination, institutional racism. Systemic racism exists within political, economic and social institutions. In electoral politics, it is expressed in New York by the policies and rhetoric of Mayor Ed Koch, who, more than any other individual was responsible for creating the climate which led to Hawkins's murder. Mayoral candidate David Dinkins correctly observed that "the Mayor sets the tide and tone with respect to race relations." Koch was more than willing to feed the flames of racial bigotry in order to secure his reelection.

Institutional racism means that young African Americans have fewer opportunities to pursue a college degree today than in the early 1970s. The system would rather incarcerate the poor and undereducated than provide the programs necessary for productive lives.

Institutional racism within the economic system today means that the rhetoric of equal opportunity in the marketplace remains a hoax for most people of color. When thousands of African-American families struggle to save enough for home mortgages and loans to start small businesses, they are frequently denied funds from banks. According to a recent study commissioned by the Federal Reserve Bank of Boston, for instance, the percentage of loans made in predominantly black communities is substantially lower than that for white neighborhoods. From 1982 to 1987, mortgages were issued on 6.9 percent of properties in white areas, but only 2.7 percent in areas which are virtually all black. By denying credit to blacks and other people of color in the central cities, this accelerates the process of gentrification, permitting thousands of middle-class whites to seize minority-owned properties at bargain-basement prices in the central cities.

The murder of Yusuf K. Hawkins highlights the terrible face of racial violence, which is the most visible manifestation of racism. But let us not forget that even if racist lynchings and shootings disappeared, the more fundamental reality of institutional racism within America's political economy and social system would still continue to challenge us.

September 1989

South Africa:
The Death of Apartheid?

We are witnessing the beginning of the death of apartheid in South Africa. The glue which has held the oppressive system of racial domination together for over 41 years has been the unity of the Afrikaner white minority, which has armed itself with the most sophisticated military weapons to ensure its survival. This month's elections in the white house of Parliament illustrate that unity of the white electorate has shattered, in the aftermath of worldwide pressure from economic divestment and political isolation. The ruling National Party, the architect of apartheid, suffered heavy losses to political rivals on the Right and Left.

The recent political crisis for white supremacy in Africa began with the forced resignation of former President P.W. Botha and the ascension to power of F.W. de Klerk as head of the Nationals. De Klerk recognized that he had to cultivate a "liberal" image if apartheid had any prospect for regaining international support and investor confidence. The remaking of apartheid's image was unveiled at the National Party congress in late June. De Klerk called for "limited power sharing" between the nation's five million whites and the 28 million oppressed and disfranchised Africans. The Nationals adopted a so-called "action plan," which called for the removal of criminal penalties for violating segregated housing laws, and expanded government support for nonwhite education. De Klerk was prepared to amputate the Party's neo-Nazi, ultra-racist right wing, which had formed the new Conservative Party, and to appeal to the more moderate sentiments of middle-class whites in the Democratic Party.

Coinciding with de Klerk's policy shift was a visit by an all-white, 115-member delegation from South Africa to Lusaka, Zambia, for meetings with the outlawed leadership of the African National Congress, headed by exiled president, Oliver Tambo and imprisoned martyr, Nelson Mandela. The majority in the white delegation was clearly unsympathetic to many of the ANC's policies, including the use of armed struggle against the apartheid regime. Most also opposed the use of economic or military sanctions against the all-white government. But on the central issue at hand—the ultimate elimination of the apartheid policy of racial segregation, and the establishment of a multi-racial democracy with full constitutional rights for people of color—the white delegation and the ANC had no disagreements. Optimistically, Tambo declared at the end of the negotiations, "Today we can truly say that the end of the apartheid system is in sight."

Why has this political change occurred within South Africa? There are several fundamental reasons for the new flexibility coming from Pretoria. International pressure against the regime, firstly, has been building since the early 1980s, despite former President Reagan's notorious policy of "Constructive Engagement" with apartheid, which aligned the United States with the domestic terrorism and brutality of the government against progressive forces. The divestment of several hundred U.S. and European firms from South Africa placed economic pressure on the government. Most of these foreign firms were capital-intensive with substantial numbers of white collar employees. Given the racial stratification of the South African labor force, divestment meant that the overwhelming number of employees whose jobs were in jeopardy were not black, but white. When American multi-nationals began to pull out, white politicians in the National Party recognized that some sort of liberalization policy was necessary to keep the economy going.

Secondly, the progressive forces of the anti-apartheid struggle resurfaced in the 1980s, with the development of the United Democratic Front in 1983 and the rapid expansion of a nonwhite, militant labor movement. Even after the apartheid regime initiated a draconian state of emergency in 1986, these progressive social forces were not completely eradicated. Thousands began to disobey apartheid laws, and it became impossible for the government to arrest and imprison them all. Although South Africa still has the highest per capita prison population in the world—the United States is second—the country's legal system could not accommodate millions of dissenters.

A third, and in many ways the most overlooked factor in South Africa's internal change has occurred because key elements of the white minority population no longer support apartheid. Significant sectors of the educated middle class, business executives and financial leaders have never been members of the National Party. Like liberal white politician Helen Suzman, they oppose the brutalities of apartheid as irrational, inefficient and anti-democratic. Clearly, they do not share the ANC's political commitment to social equality, which would require the economic redistribution of power and ownership in a post-apartheid state. But they also have no intention of sitting silently on a white, racist Titanic, as the ship of state slips into the waters. Key groups of moderate whites are searching desperately for a strategy which will guarantee a sort of Zimbabwean solution—black and Indian domination of the political system with a multi-party democracy, and continued white domination of the banks, industry, land and investment.

The harsh reality of "moderate apartheid" was also apparent during recent weeks, with the unjustified arrest of Nobel prize winner Archbishop Desmond Tutu in Cape Town, and the arrest and beating of thousands of anti-apartheid protestors from religious, labor, and educational groups. In Durban, over 200 medical students were arrested by police in protests. In Cape Town and other cities, police used heavy whips, tear gas, rubber bullets and occasionally live ammunition to break up nonviolent demonstrations.

The recent events inside South Africa also represent a larger international struggle against race/class domination. Former President Ronald Reagan was the chief political ally and supporter of the apartheid regime. His policy toward apartheid, dubbed "Constructive Engagement," meant, in effect, support for expanded U.S. investment inside South Africa, while saying virtually nothing critical of the regime's massive violations of human rights. George Bush is pursuing a more sophisticated strategy, which recognizes that apartheid will self-destruct within the next decade, and that civil relations have to be established with the black-majority leadership which will emerge into power. Consequently, this June, Bush met at the White House with Albertina Sisulu, co-president of the United Democratic Front, the country's largest anti-apartheid formation.

Simultaneously, however, both Bush and South African apartheid leader F.W. de Klerk are striving to alter the image of the regime as being more moderate. Members of the Bush administration state that de Klerk is "more willing" to negotiate with African leaders on measures to dismantle apartheid. Herman J. Cohen, the Assistant Secretary of State for African Affairs, states that de Klerk "ought to be given a chance...We'll wait and see what he does." For his part, de Klerk has endeavored to project a flexible stance toward some type of black participation in a new future legislature.

Nevertheless, the bestial realities of apartheid have not changed. When de Klerk announced the new liberalization policies of the ruling National Party, he also added that the two central laws of apartheid—the Group Areas Act, creating racially segregated districts, and the Population Registration Act, which tracks all people by "racial classification"—will never be overturned. The illusion of reform is fostered, but not the reality. For example, early this year when hundreds of political prisoners initiated a hunger strike, the regime released nearly 1,000 under "restriction orders." They were "free" to live under house arrest with their families. Technically, the anti-apartheid protestors had been released, yet their activities continued to be closely monitored by authorities and their telephones tapped.

What practical steps can be taken to accelerate the inevitable democratization of South Africa and the demise of apartheid? First, and foremost, is the continuing campaign for divestment. Last month, the leaders of the Evangelical Lutheran Church in America voted to divest $85 million in pension money in companies which still conduct business inside South Africa. The 5.3 million-member denomination's action was not unexpected. Forty-four of the 65 regional synods of the Evangelical Lutherans had previously demanded the total divestment from apartheid-related corporations, but they had not set firm deadlines. The new action set a two-year timetable, and represented a sharp challenge to other religious groups which have not yet divested their holdings in South Africa. Religious organizations, churches and synagogues must be forced to confront this issue at every opportunity, calling into question the ethics of receiving profits from human misery and exploitation.

But perhaps the most important role we can play in accelerating the struggle for democracy inside South Africa is to ensure that this issue remains in the forefront of public policy debates inside the United States. Students have an obligation to demand academic courses and workshops on the issue of apartheid, and to demand that their university regents or trustees divest holdings from firms which continue to do business in South Africa. We should encourage the selective use of nonviolent, civil disobedience, blocking the entrances of banks, corporations and religious institutions with apartheid investments. The Bush administration has absolutely no commitment to majority rule inside South Africa. By increasing our political pressure in this country, we can push the apartheid regime toward meaningful negotiations with the forces of progressive change.

September 1989

Freedom for Namibia

In only two months, an election will be held in Namibia which could decide the future of the entire liberation struggle throughout Southern Africa. An international agreement sponsored by the United Nations has created the possibility for democracy and majority rule for this southwest African state, which has been controlled by white South Africa for decades. But the promise of democratic government is being threatened by several factors, which may yet produce the tyranny of white supremacy throughout the region.

South Africa accepted this international election in Namibia due largely to events which began back in 1976. Apartheid troops were defeated militarily by the Angolans and Cubans in Angola's liberation war. South Africa suffered serious strategic losses also with the independence of Mozambique; and within another four years, Zimbabwe would be liberated as well. Consequently, the South Africans fell back on Namibia as their last line of defense. The South African air force constructed a series of bases along the northern frontier of Namibia, and conducted bombing raids against the South West African People's Organization (SWAPO) camps in Angola. In 1978, the apartheid military escalated these attacks, and in one instance the South African air force murdered over 600 civilians in one bombing raid.

It was in response to the apartheid assault that the United Nations called for a peace plan in 1978, which included an immediate cease fire; the removal of all but 1,500 South African troops after two months; and the scheduling of elections for a new constituent assembly based on universal suffrage. Under the Carter administration, South Africa was being pressured to accept these terms; but after the U.S. elections of 1980, the Reagan administration informed the apartheid regime that they were under no pressure to accept the UN's agreement immediately. The United States used its diplomatic weight to permit South Africa to consolidate itself inside Namibia, by establishing paramilitary forces among the white settler population, and by recruiting blacks who accepted a puppet/client role in opposition to SWAPO.

The South Africans were only forced to come to terms in 1988, when they were defeated militarily at the battle of Cuito Cuanavale. It had become clear to them that Namibia could no longer be held as a direct colony of apartheid. But the Reagan administration had given the South Africans eight important years in which to consolidate its clients inside Namibia. They were able to recruit spies and agents to infiltrate SWAPO; and they had identified local blacks who were agreeable to oppose SWAPO in the upcoming constituent elections.

Although the international agreement declares that the people of Namibia must exercise self-determination, South Africa has a strategy to undermine this process. According to a provision in the agreement, any white South Africans who were born in Namibia or who can prove at least four years' residency will be permitted to vote in the Namibian election, even if they no longer live in the country. The apartheid regime has registered perhaps as many as 150,000 whites in an effort to throw the election from the black majority. Most political observers had assumed that SWAPO, which has been the leading progressive political force in the struggle against apartheid domination of the country, would easily win more than the two-thirds electoral support required to control the new constituent assembly. But a combination of errors and mistakes on the part of SWAPO, plus the maneuverings of the apartheid regime and its local allies, now have created a giant question mark for Namibia's future.

SWAPO's first error occurred in April, immediately preceding the initiation of the UN peace settlement process. SWAPO ordered into northern Namibia perhaps as many as 1,200 fighters of its People's Liberation Army of Namibia. The purpose was to consolidate its position in the region. South Africa's military and its local paramilitary clients reacted, killing 300 fighters, and terrorizing the local population. This permitted the South Africans to delay the process of demilitarization until mid-August. During this interim period, the military and paramilitary units were able to intimidate thousands of potential voters. African voters were told to stay away from political meetings sponsored by SWAPO, and not to register for the elections. In the northern part of the country, where the greatest fighting occurred this year, registration figures are very low—in precisely the electoral areas which SWAPO had counted on to produce its necessary 66 percent mandate.

SWAPO's second political error was the product of South Africa's successful attempts to infiltrate the organization over a period of several years. Under the terms of the independence process, both the apartheid regime and SWAPO were obligated to release their detainees. Hundreds of SWAPO prisoners were indeed agents of apartheid. But unfortunately, many others were not. SWAPO officials now admit that many mistakes were made in the treatment of prisoners, and that those individuals who have acted against party procedures will be held accountable and prosecuted. However, the entire incident has created the sense among many supporters of SWAPO that the organization has lost a good amount of political credibility.

A third mistake is that of political inconsistency. SWAPO for many years maintained an unambiguous political line, calling for a fundamental, radical economic reorganization of the nation, and a sharp break from all commercial ties with apartheid. But SWAPO has modified its economic program in an attempt to win over non-

SWAPO constituencies. This effort has confused their core defenders.

If SWAPO fails to win a two-thirds vote, the liberation struggle may be stalled for another decade or more. But the forces of white supremacy are taking no chances. On 12 September, for example, one of the senior white officials of SWAPO, Anton Lubowski, an attorney and former member of the South African army who defected to the Africans, was murdered in front of his home in Windhoek. Lubowski would have become a key leader of a SWAPO-led government. When pushed to the limit, apartheid and its clients in Namibia respond with terror, harassment and death. These are the essential tools of racism.

South Africa cannot achieve freedom unless Namibia also becomes free. We must pressure the Bush administration to step up tougher sanctions against South Africa. We should also contact Congresspeople Howard Wolpe (D) and Dan Burton (R), the chair and ranking Republican members, respectively, of the House Foreign Affairs Subcommittee on Africa, to demand the end of South Africa's murderous maneuvers to subvert majority rule and democracy in Namibia.

October 1989

South Africa: What Next?

In the aftermath of Nelson Mandela's release from prison, the South African system of apartheid has reached the beginning of its end. Last month, one white government official predicted that the dictatorship of white minority rule would disappear within five years. The Broederbond, the powerful Afrikaner secret society, has reconciled itself to the future domination by the black majority, but is still desperately attempting to establish "structural guarantees" to preserve white privileges.

Mandela's liberation has caused many white Western observers to praise and embrace the actions of apartheid boss F.W. de Klerk, calling this white supremacist a "South African version of Mikhail Gorbachev." Chester A. Crocker, Reagan's Assistant Secretary of State for African Affairs, recently repeated such nonsense in the *New York Times:* "de Klerk's new thinking (indicates) a readiness to listen to diverse views...he represents the younger Afrikaner political generation, which learned the lessons of the 1980's and watched in frustration as former leaders wasted one golden opportunity after another." The effort is to present de Klerk as some type of liberal statesman, despite his regime's record of human rights crimes against black people. One does not thank a political sadist who puts away his well-worn whip after bloodying the backs of countless victims, because his arm is tired.

South Africa released Mandela, in part, because it has surrendered all political and moral credibility in the world, and even among many of its own white citizens. A quarter of the white electorate last year voted for a liberal party committed to ending the apartheid system.

South Africa's white economic elite, those who control the major banks and businesses, have been forced to the negotiating table because of the power of sanctions.

The South African Reserve Bank had a short-term debt of $8 billion to Western financial institutions, plus billions more indebtedness in long-term obligations. South Africa owes $2.4 billion to American banks alone. Seven American companies divested from apartheid in 1984, at the beginning of the divestment campaign here in the United States. In 1987, 56 U.S. corporations departed. By 1990, over 350 firms had cut direct ties with South Africa, and roughly one-half of this number had also cut off any indirect associations, such as licensing agreements or arrangements to export South African products.

Under economic pressure, South Africa's white population experienced spiralling unemployment and a reduction in their purchasing power. The value of apartheid's currency plummeted. In February, when Nelson Mandela was released, and he reasserted the ANC's long-held objective of nationalization of key industries, the Johannesburg Stock Exchange Overall Index dropped 7.5 percent in only three days. International Investors, Inc., the largest gold fund for Americans who invest in South Africa's gold industry, declined 13 percent in only one week. Foreign investors, bankers and many white-held corporations are frightened by the economic instability and uncertainty which is forcing the apartheid regime to seek some kind of negotiated peace with the ANC.

Recent international events have also influenced the strategy of liberation forces toward South Africa. The liberation of Namibia in 1989, under the leadership of the South West Africa People's Organization (SWAPO), increased the African National Congress's bargaining power. But another factor which affected the ANC was the radical shift in the Soviet Union's foreign policy under Mikhail Gorbachev. The revolutions in Eastern Europe and the process of democratization within the Soviet Union have contributed to a fundamental rethinking of communists' attitudes toward the entire third world. In the mid-1980s, the Soviets used their influence to force

Angola and Cuba to negotiate with the South Africans, leading to the departure of Cuban troops from Angola. The Soviets also supported the United Nations' efforts in Namibia to reach a negotiated settlement.

For decades, the Soviets trained and armed ANC guerrillas, and provided diplomatic muscle as well. Diplomatic relations between the Soviet Union and South Africa were severed in 1956. But now the Soviets are advancing a strategy of compromise, in the hope that apartheid can be negotiated out of existence. Boris Asoyan, a top Soviet expert on Southern Africa, stated in early 1989: "In our opinion, we doubt that revolution in South Africa is possible, if you're talking of revolutionaries storming Pretoria. We support the ANC...but we also believe that there is really no alternative to a peaceful solution." Soviet scholars at Moscow's African Institute are now saying that there must be willingness to compromise in providing "security for all racial groups, whites as well as blacks." Moscow has pulled the plug on its support for military actions against apartheid, and is now prepared to reestablish diplomatic relations once official talks between Pretoria and the ANC begin.

However, the fundamental driving force of progressive change inside South Africa has always been, and remains, the masses of oppressed African people, the chief victims of the terror and brutality which is essential for apartheid's survival. As Nelson Mandela observed upon his release: "It is not the kings and generals that make history, but the masses of the people." What has motivated these countless women and men to make such sacrifices, to bury their sons and daughters, mowed down by police bullets and clubs, to engage in economic boycotts, to burn their pass books?

They fight, and continue to fight, for a powerful democratic ideal, a government and society without institutional violence and racism. As Mandela wisely observed: "The fears of whites about their rights and place in a South Africa they do not control exclusively are an obstacle we must understand and address...(The ANC and I) are opposed to black domination and white domination. We must accept that our statements and declarations alone will not be sufficient to allay the fears of white South Africans. We must clearly demonstrate our good will to our white compatriots and convince them by our conduct...that a South Africa without apartheid will be a better home for all." South Africa without apartheid would be a productive and fertile land, a nation of wealth, education and culture. A democracy without racism, inferior schools, police terrorism and surveillance, segregated residential districts and economic inequality, is the vision which can become a reality, but only with continued struggle.

April 1990

Apartheid:
The Fight's Not Finished

In a major parliamentary address last month, South African president F.W. de Klerk announced the repeal of the last major elements of apartheid. Calling for the "elimination of racial discrimination" and the abolition of "injustice" and "tyranny," de Klerk called for the abolition of the Group Areas Act, which limits where nonwhites are permitted to live; the Land Acts of 1913 and 1936, which allocated 87 percent of the nation's land to whites; and the Population Registration Act, which categorized all people into strict racial groups and limited the rights and privileges of all nonwhites. The abolition of these repressive and anti-democratic provisions would establish the basis for constructing a real democracy.

De Klerk was widely praised for these bold pronouncements. And, in fact, the parliamentary walkout staged by the right-wing Conservative Party in protest of de Klerk's speech only reinforced the sharp break with legal racism which the President's address represented. This was the culmination of a series of governmental reforms over the past twelve months. In February 1990, the African National Congress was unbanned, and ANC leader Nelson Mandela was freed from prison. In May 1990, hospitals were technically opened to all ethnic groups. Last October, the Separate Amenities Act was repealed, which ended the legal basis for racial segregation in many public places. In February 1991, government officials announced that parents would no longer be required to state the race of their newborn infants when registering births.

The Bush administration was quick to announce de Klerk's speech as "dramatic and far-reaching."

Apartheid's old friends inside the U.S. Congress and corporate community called for an end to sanctions against the regime. U.S. businesses began to speak of reinvesting inside South Africa, and announced the death of the "divestment" movement.

Has the leopard really changed its spots? What is actually occurring inside South Africa is a desperate attempt by the white establishment to consolidate its power and privileges, while simultaneously transforming its political system to permit nonwhite participation, and even the probability of a black president. Three years ago, then-President P.W. Botha announced the start of an official "privatization" program, which would sell off government-owned monopolies to white corporations. In October 1989, the regime sold its Iron and Steel Corporation (ISCOR) to private interests for over $1.4 billion. To foster the development of a petty capitalist class among Africans, the government announced its intention to sell its breweries for African-style sorghum beer to blacks.

This rush toward privatization represents a sharp repudiation of past governmental policies by the ruling whites. Despite pro-capitalist rhetoric, the apartheid regime developed a series of powerful state-owned monopolies, including railroads, airports, telecommunications, petroleum pipelines, television and radio stations, and harbors. Now that the specter of black domination of the government looms, whites want to push government-owned assets into private hands.

More ominously, South Africa has not moved to reform the system in all aspects. Many political prisoners still languish behind bars, more than one year after Mandela's release. Two weeks after de Klerk's address, the South African police arrested 11,000 people in a two-day period. Although the mass arrests were declared to focus on violent crime, the ANC questioned the regime's motives and called for a breakdown by race of all prisoners.

The struggle to abolish apartheid has two phases. The first phase, which is the outlawing of all discriminatory laws, is nearly completed. The second stage, the establishment of a political and economic democracy, in which all citizens have opportunities for development, is just beginning. The struggle to free South Africa isn't finished, and we have a political and moral responsibility to make sure that the Bush administration doesn't embrace the so-called "reforms" as the final phase of democracy inside South Africa.

March 1991

The New International Racism

A generation ago, "racism" during the Jim Crow segregation era meant "white" and "colored" signs indicating a separate and unequal status for people of color. But today, throughout the Western capitalist world, we are witnessing a new kind of racism, rooted in the changing ethnic and socioeconomic realities of the post-Cold War period. There is a link, in short, between President Bush's veto of the Civil Rights Act of 1990, the solid majority given by white voters to David Duke in his unsuccessful campaign for senator of Louisiana, and the international discrimination and oppression against nonwhite immigrants and undocumented refugees.

Throughout the Western world in recent years, there has been a dramatic upsurge in the politics of racism, including vigilante violence, aimed at people of color or ethnic minorities. In France, the neo-fascist National Front has campaigned successfully on the issue of white supremacy. The Front's leader deliberately provoked racist assaults on nonwhites by calling openly for Arabs, Africans and other "foreigners" to be expelled back to "their caves on the other side of the Mediterranean." More than 100 North Africans living in France were killed by whites in a 12-year period. Despite the liberal rhetoric of the socialist Mitterand government, people of color experience deportation, identity checks by police, and legal harassment.

In Italy, dozens of black small merchants and workers have been assaulted in Milan and Turin this year. Pamphlets have been circulated calling for the construction of "crematoriums for immigrants and Jews." A new racist political party has been formed, the Lombardy League, with the goal of recruiting low-income, working-class whites and first-time voters. Similar developments have occurred in the Netherlands with the establishment of the Centrum Party, which advocates racist policies.

But the most dramatic examples of racism are occurring in Great Britain. Hundreds of people of color, of Asian, African and Caribbean ancestry, have been victims of racially-motivated violence. Conservative Prime Minister Margaret Thatcher has warned that she would never permit England to be "swamped by people with a different culture." In 1981, Parliament passed the Nationality Act, which ended the ancient definition of citizenship as based on one's birth on British soil, and instead placed it on an individual's descent or patrilineage.

How do we explain this rise of racial bigotry and violence within European societies? European and American corporations destroyed third world traditional economies, creating millions of unemployed, landless people. Western governments created authoritarian regimes in these countries which would protect capitalist investments, control trade unions, and eliminate radical protest. Thus, millions of nonwhite people began to move to the white West in search of jobs and opportunity.

By 1986, about 7 percent of the populations of the Netherlands, France and West Germany were ethnic minorities. Immigrants comprise 14.5 percent of Switzerland's population. Millions of African and Asian people live and work in London, Paris, and Europe's other major cities. Immigrants of color are allocated their society's worst and most hazardous jobs. In West Germany, for example, Turks are widely viewed as "subhuman." German subcontractors have been known to hire out Turkish workers on a temporary basis to clean up nuclear power plants so that the workers return home before the radiation takes effect.

The new racism is necessary to justify the exploitation and discrimination of whites over nonwhites. But an even greater factor is fear. By the year 2050, there will be a projected eleven billion people worldwide. Only 1.4

billion of them will live in the United States, Canada, Europe and Japan, the industrialized, wealthy nations. The vast majority of humankind will be nonwhite, as is already the case. Even ten years from today, Sao Paulo, Brazil will have a population of 30 million; Rio de Janeiro, Cairo and Mexico City will exceed 20 million. The fundamental political reality of the twenty-first century will be the struggle for equality and democracy between the white "North" and the impoverished, exploited, nonwhite "South."

November 1990

Why Blacks Feel Threatened

Several days ago, a Philadelphia newspaper editor suggested that black welfare mothers should be "encouraged" to stop reproducing sexually, by implanting in their arms the new five-year birth control device. To many African Americans, this was yet one more indication that the black community was under attack, targeted by a new, more sophisticated form of white racism.

In politics, the Bush administration ignored the advice of prominent black Republicans, such as former Secretary of Transportation William T. Coleman and Secretary of Health and Human Services Louis Sullivan, by vetoing the 1990 Civil Rights Bill. The excuse given by Bush—that the legislation made it too difficult for employers to defend themselves against charges of racism—in effect appealed to the white supremacist wing of the Republican Party. On this issue, Bush was closer to David Duke than the majority of Americans.

The ink on the vetoed bill was barely dry before the next racial controversy, the new policy which would deny federal funds to colleges which awarded scholarships to minority students on the basis of race. Black and Latino educators pointed out that colleges had allocated special scholarships for decades to athletes and others with special skills. Nearly all scholarships for minority students were not based narrowly on race, but on economic need as well as other important criteria. The sharp reaction against this new policy forced Bush into a quick turnabout, declaring that scholarships specifically for racial minorities could be drawn from private funds. But in effect, the entire episode implied that blacks, hispanics and other people of color should be excluded from higher education.

For African Americans, these two incidents seemed to symbolize the end of an entire historical period, the civil rights movement for democracy in America. For many years, a sense of optimism and hope pervaded black politics. The movement from racial segregation to full participation within the American mainstream was taken for granted. Now, all the evidence points to a deterioration in the economic and social status of blacks in American life, and the Bush administration seems willing to push minorities over the abyss.

For example, in terms of health care, an alarming gap has been created between African Americans and whites. According to the National Center for Health Statistics, the life expectancy for black men has fallen to 64.9 years, below retirement age. Another recent health study found that blacks, who represent only 13 percent of the total U.S. population, now account for 80 percent of all premature deaths—that is, deaths of individuals between the ages of 15 and 44—because of abnormally high rates of pneumonia, asthma, bladder infections, and other diseases. Blacks, hispanics and low-income people die sooner than upper-class whites, because they have no access to regular health care services and because many have no health insurance.

Economically, the same picture of inequality emerges. The recent failure of Harlem's Freedom National Bank, one of the largest minority-owned financial institutions in the country, revealed that the government was unwilling to bail out economically distressed institutions when they held blacks' funds. As the recession deepens, the jobless rates in the black community have soared, while the Bush administration does nothing.

What all these elements have in common is the phony concept of "reverse racism," that blacks have been given too much over the years. The only way to reverse these trends is to rebuild the black protest movement, to challenge the system which perpetuates inequality.

January 1991

Chapter VI

America's
One Party System

Reagan's Racial Fantasy

For eight years, former President Ronald Reagan was the chief advocate of racial inequality in America. Reagan never pulled the Klansman's sheets from his political closet. He never engaged in the obnoxious political demagoguery of George Wallace or Lester "Axhandle" Maddox. But more than any other white politician of the post-civil rights era, he successfully brought together a conservative political ideology of limited federal government, lower taxes and *laissez faire* economics, with a conservative racial ideology of undermining affirmative action and equal opportunity legislation.

Reagan was the architect of what can be termed "nonracist racism." Superficially, Reagan's utterances on race relations don't seem to be overtly discriminatory. He never stood defiantly at the schoolhouse door, challenging federal authorities on the issue of black access to public higher education. He never publicly applauded the racist brutalities of the apartheid regime, calling instead for a vague "constructive engagement" with the criminals at the head of South Africa. Reagan went so far as to appoint a Negro to his presidential cabinet, even though by all accounts he became the least effective and most ignored official in Reagan's administration.

But with a fine instinct for the political gutter, Reagan sensed that there was political capital to be made by cultivating the backlash of low-to-middle-income whites against the achievements of the civil rights struggle. Reagan's view of the world, in terms of race relations, was frozen during the Great Depression, pre-World War II period. This was a time in which no blacks were permitted to participate in professional sports; when there was only one black representative in Congress, and no elected black mayors anywhere in the country; when the black middle class was virtually nonexistent; and when Jim Crow segregation laws were permanent barriers to blacks' socioeconomic mobility.

Consistently, the former president blamed blacks for their own oppression. When cutting child nutrition programs, public housing and medical care, he crudely blamed those who were on the periphery of despair and starvation for their social marginality. He assured the white middle class that the concentration of wealth in the hands of the rich was the greatest guarantee for protecting the rights of the poor. In brief, Reagan understood that the ideological glue for his motley set of reactionary policies was racial inequality. By keeping the poor divided on racial lines, the vast majority of Americans would continue to be fooled and manipulated by the Far Right's destructive policies.

In the twilight of his administration, Reagan could not resist twisting the rhetorical knife in the backs of the black community's leadership. Reagan insisted in a recent interview that oppressed blacks were being misled by civil rights leaders and organizations, and that prominent black Americans, such as NAACP head Benjamin Hooks and Jesse Jackson distorted his public record on race relations. "Sometimes I wonder if they really want what they say they want," Reagan declared, "because some of those leaders are doing very well leading organizations based on keeping alive the feeling that they're victims of prejudice."

Civil rights leaders quickly and correctly condemned Reagan's latest political broadside. Jesse Jackson responded that Reagan "never saw a piece of civil rights legislation that he would stand up for." Civil rights lawyer and historian Mary Frances Berry termed Reagan's remarks "vacuous." But the reality behind Reagan's assertion is a political effort to turn back the political clock, to the days of segregated water fountains, buses and public schools. Reagan's racial fantasy is to blame black leaders for the oppression of African Americans, while reinforcing racial inequality within the economy and society. President Bush's racial agenda is less crude, perhaps, but is equally repressive.

February 1989

The Republicans
and White Racism

The recent controversy concerning the election of ex-Ku Klux Klan leader David Duke to the Louisiana State Legislature has provoked considerable polemics from the leaders of the national Republican Party. Since Duke ran for office successfully as a Republican, and has a long history of racist and anti-Semitic agitation, the Republicans are obviously fearful that their tenuous links to racial minorities and more substantial ties to conservative Jewish organizations could be damaged.

Lee Atwater, the national Republican Party chairman, attacked Duke as a "charlatan" and demanded that the party's National Executive Committee censure him. Ex-President Reagan made commercials for Duke's opponent, and local GOP officials scrambled to distance themselves from their own victorious candidate. The Democrats generally ridiculed Republican efforts to disavow Duke, noting that the election of a Klansman was only the logical culmination of the GOP's entire political strategy in the Deep South. Representative Tony Coelho, the House democratic whip, reflected that Duke's triumph at the polls illustrated that "Republicans had gone too far" in manipulating racism for electoral purposes. "Now you have the Republicans saying, 'Oh Lordy, Lordy, Lordy, isn't this terrible.' Well, they were playing with matches, they were playing with fire."

Coelho's explanation is partially correct. But to understand Duke's victory, one must first examine the evolution of racial politics within both major parties over the past thirty years.

Throughout most of its history, the Democratic Party was essentially the party of white supremacy. Southern

Democrats, termed "Dixiecrats," dominated the party's power elites. Eastern Republicans like Wilkie, Dewey, and later, Senators Lowell Weiker of Connecticut, Charles Percy of Illinois, and New York's Jacob Javits were far more "liberal" on civil rights concerns than most Democrats. The ideological realignment on race began to occur by the 1960s, as African Americans assumed a major role in the success of the Democratic Party's electoral efforts. The majority of white Americans voted against John Kennedy in 1960 and Jimmy Carter in 1976—but the black electorate's solid support swept both Democratic presidential candidates into the White House. As the national leadership of the Democratic Party began to favor antidiscrimination laws, affirmative action, expanded social welfare programs and minority economic set-asides, larger numbers of African Americans shifted from the Republican to the Democratic Party.

White Southern Democrats reacted to their party's "liberalization" on the race issue by mounting an electoral protest led by Alabama Governor George Wallace in the 1960s and early 1970s. Wallace's revolt was anti-black, to be sure, but it was also ideologically reactionary on many issues which had nothing directly to do with race relations *per sé*. Wallace used vulgar race-baiting as a technique to win the allegiance of poor and working-class whites behind a reactionary political program.

In the 1980 election, Reagan perfected Wallace's southern strategy by advancing a more sophisticated version of racism. Reagan had openly opposed the 1964 Civil Rights Act and the 1965 Voting Rights Act. He publicly embraced the slogan "State's Rights," a code word for southern segregation. But he didn't personally block black children from entering public schools; and he didn't applaud the Klan or vigilante violence against nonwhites. Reagan acted through symbols, rather than through overt actions. But by destroying the Civil Rights Commission, condemning affirmative action and the goals of equal opportunity, Reagan sent an unambiguous message of support for white supremacy's ideal of separate and unequal. Most Dixiecrats joined the Republican Party as hard-line Reaganites, and denounced the GOP's older liberal tradition favoring civil rights. They also tended to favor socially conservative goals, such as anti-abortion legislation, school prayer, and the death penalty.

Last year, George Bush's campaign deliberately provoked racist fears among whites. Conservative white Republicans regularly used thinly veiled code-words to identify the Democrats as the "party of the blacks." Lee Atwater was the chief architect of this sophisticated racism. GOP candidates consistently attacked Democrats' positions on welfare spending, job programs, school busing to achieve racial integration, and crime issues in a calculated effort to mobilize racist forces within the electorate.

Since most Americans no longer accept the crude racism of a George Wallace, the Republicans are forced to carry out their gutter campaign by maintaining a nominal posture of racial tolerance. The Republicans stepped up efforts to recruit black middle-class and professional people. Atwater claimed several weeks ago that "A lot of blacks are tired of being taken for granted by the Democrats." In Florida, the state's Republican organization initiated "Operation Inclusion" with various black communities, and plans to spend $150,000 starting black GOP political clubs.

Despite the denials of Bush, Atwater, and company, the election of Duke in Louisiana is the inevitable result of the Republicans' twenty-year strategy to become a national white united front. Blacks who claim that the Republican Party's approach to racial issues is rooted in a respect for civil rights are only fooling themselves. Duke proclaims publicly what Reagan and hundreds of white Republican legislators, committeemen, and party activists say privately in their country clubs and board rooms.

Duke is embarrassing because he reveals the dirty truth about the Republican ascendancy in presidential politics since 1968. White racism is absolutely central to the rise of Reaganism and white political conservatism.

March 1989

No Glory for Old Glory

One of the most controversial Supreme Court decisions in years was the recent ruling which affirmed the
protest act of burning the American flag as a protected
form of free speech. By a narrow five-to-four majority, the
high court declared that flag burning may be a detestable
act, but it is nevertheless an expressive conduct protected
by the First Amendment to the Constitution. "We do not
consecrate the flag by punishing its desecration," declared
the court, "for in doing so we dilute the freedom that this
cherished emblem represents." Significantly, the ruling
was supported by two conservative justices appointed by
former President Reagan.

The politicians scaled the heights of political demagoguery in denouncing the Supreme Court's decision. In
last year's presidential election, George Bush utilized the
phony issue of mandating the pledge of allegiance in
schools to smear Democratic challenger Michael Dukakis
as "unpatriotic." Bush was quick to declare his criticism
of the recent ruling, stating his "personal, emotional"
belief that "flag burning is dead wrong."

In a rare display of bipartisan unity, Republicans
and Democrats clamored to display their patriotism.
House Speaker Tom Foley declared that "Americans look
on the burning of the American flag with abhorrence, and
it is deeply offensive to virtually all Americans, and it will
be a difficult matter for them to understand how it can be
justified under any circumstances." Republican Congressman Ron Marlenee of Montana reminded his colleagues
of the flag-bearing soldiers depicted at the Marine Corps
memorial and declared that "those six brave soldiers were
symbolically shot in the back." Democratic Congressman
Doug Applegate fumed that the justices had "humiliated"

the flag, and wondered aloud, "Are they going to allow fornication in Times Square at high noon?"

Even more irrational and jingoistic were conservative ideologues, who felt betrayed by the Reaganites on the Supreme Court who inexplicably voted with the few remaining liberal justices. Former Nixon speechwriter and conservative journalist Patrick Buchanan was livid. "The Supreme Court has turned a hate crime into a constitutional argument," Buchanan stated. "They don't understand the meaning of the flag." In Buchanan's opinion, the ruling "is an invitation to civil war, when you undermine the symbolism" of the American flag.

Should the public burning of "Old Glory," the Stars and Stripes, merit a prison sentence? More than two out of three Americans polled oppose the Supreme Court's insistence that the First Amendment rights of those who reject the government and its flag had to be preserved. Nevertheless, the high court's ruling was correct, although I would advance different reasons to preserve the right of those who choose to destroy the flag as a form of political protest.

The flag is not symbolic of the heritage of the entire people, but rather a civil icon of the federal government. Should any state punish dissenters for attacking symbols of the government as an act of protest? Suppose Soviet dissidents gathered in Moscow's Red Square and burned the government's red flag? If Soviet authorities imprisoned the protestors, the same American politicians in both parties would demagogically insist upon the release of the prisoners. If pro-Contra demonstrators burned the Sandinista flag in Managua, Buchanan would be praising them. Why is the American flag any different? No government should have the right to imprison or punish those who reject its banners or symbols, whether the icons are stars and stripes, or hammers and sickles.

Where do you draw the line in prohibiting legitimate protest? A constitutional amendment could be passed to outlaw the burning of the flag. Would artists' paintings which used the flag in a critical manner also be forbidden? Perhaps there would be a demand to outlaw any political demonstrations which burned models of the Statue of Liberty, or photographs of the president. Within a few years, we might be jailed for writing letters to newspapers which criticized U.S. policies.

What does Old Glory really represent to millions of Americans who have experienced racism, unemployment, poverty, and homelessness? The Stars and Stripes flew over slave markets where black families were permanently divided. It was unfurled at the massacre of Wounded Knee in 1890, when hundreds of Native Americans were slaughtered. It flew from public buildings which were segregated by law for decades. The flag was carried into illegal and immoral military operations from Vietnam to Grenada. There's no glory in Old Glory for those who have been deliberately denied the American Dream. And as long as equality and justice are illusions for millions of people, the flag will be an ironic reminder of absence of real democracy in this country.

Protestors who burn the flag, however, do not advance the struggle for democracy, because they create easy and emotional targets for public outrage. Instead of burning the flag, we need to challenge the political system it represents in order to achieve economic opportunity and social justice for all.

July 1989

America's One Party System

The greatest political problem confronting black America and other people of color is the fact that we lack any effective democracy to empower ourselves to address our problems of poverty, unemployment, poor health care, and urban deterioration. As the entire world apparently is moving toward greater democracy in its political systems, especially in South Africa and Eastern Europe, we are burdened with a two party system which either represents us poorly, or not at all. With a few significant exceptions, notably the Congressional Black Caucus and local officials, too many white Democrats have joined with the Republicans to forge a one party system, designed to protect the interests of the upper classes at our expense.

As the majority of America's white electorate shifted from the cities to the suburbs after World War II, the social base for the traditional liberal policies of the New Deal gradually collapsed. Organized labor's influence with the Democratic Party declined. Traditionally liberal constituencies such as Jewish Americans became more conservative ideologically as they moved up the social class ladder. Consequently, as white voters became more elitist, candidates for public office increasingly projected their legislative agendas in the context of local prerogatives rather than the larger, national interest. The relative clout of both parties was sharply reduced in the process.

By the 1980s, a rough division of labor existed between Republicans and Democrats. The Republicans succeeded in projecting themselves as the party of "national management," capable of running the executive branch of the federal government and making decisions in foreign policy. Since the election of Eisenhower in 1952, Republicans won the presidency seven out of ten times, and since

1968, five out of six times. White upper-middle-class Americans generally trusted the Republicans to reduce federal taxes, decrease government regulations, expand opportunities for business at the expense of working people, and to push back the demands of so-called "special interests": African Americans, hispanics, organized labor, feminists, and other political and ethnic dissidents. It is no accident that, since 1948, a majority of the white American electorate has voted for a white Democratic presidential candidate only once—Lyndon Johnson in 1964. It is no aberration that 66 percent of all white voters endorsed Reagan's reelection in 1984, or that about three-fourths of all whites holding college degrees and earning above $50,000 annually supported George Bush in 1988. Class and racial interests coincide with conservative political behavior.

The Democrats are perceived as the party of "parochial interest,"the politicians best equipped to promote the narrow prerogatives of local business and middle-to-working-class constituencies. Because Democrats still control most state legislatures and a majority of the governorships, they are able to gerrymander Congressional districts to maximize their candidates' viability. Legislative incumbents have many built-in advantages, such as free media exposure, government-subsidized mailings to constituents, and the generous support, by corporations, of their political action committees. Not surprisingly, the reelection rate of the House of Representatives was 98 percent in 1986 and 1988. With the exception of losing control of the Senate for six years during the Reagan administration, Democrats have controlled both houses of Congress for a generation.

Why are African Americans still far from achieving equality, despite the passage of civil rights legislation? Because both political parties have a vested interest in maintaining the "one party system," which is why the Democrats have ceased to function as a legitimate "opposition party" in anything but name. The Democrats recognize that they can win the presidency only by the route suggested by Jesse Jackson—expanding the base of the electorate to include millions of low-income, unemployed, minority, and working-class people who frequently stay away from voting. The Democrats would have to advance an American-styled agenda for social justice, calling for comprehensive legislation to restrict the corporations, to expanding educational, housing and health care resources, and to empower people of color. Their pathetic refusal to do so reveals that they would rather have George Bush in the White House than take the necessary steps to uproot racism, poverty, hunger and joblessness.

May 1990

What Happened
to the Liberals?

When the end of the Cold War was declared by both the Soviets and Americans, most of my political friends were overjoyed. After all, they were on the Left, and it was difficult to distinguish to a mass audience between their advocacy of policies such as full employment, reductions in the Pentagon budget, women's rights, affirmative action and increased social welfare spending from the views of "communists." In a country fed for 40 years on the sterile rhetoric of Joe McCarthy, Richard Nixon and Ronald "Evil Empire" Reagan, anything left of center was smeared as the brainchild of the "International Communist Conspiracy."

The end of hostilities with Russia meant that American progressives no longer had to explain that their opposition to the massive nuclear and conventional weapons arsenal of the United States wasn't "un-American"; that our belief in a job as a human right for all wasn't "sinister"; and that our opposition and criticisms of American military adventurism abroad, from Grenada to Lebanon wasn't "unpatriotic." Progressive politics would surely benefit from the projected peace dividend, the savings generated by reductions in Pentagon expenditures, and the peaceful economic conversion from bombs to human needs would reconstruct our central cities and poorest areas.

Alas, our hopes for transcending the politics of banality, nurtured by the stupidity of conservatives, was fatally flawed by two factors. First, the international axis of world politics suddenly shifted from east-west to north-south. The conflict with Iraq has been used to justify continued military expenditures, forgetting about all the waste, graft and corruption which is endemic to the business of arms production. Saddam Hussein has become the convenient justification for the militarism and reactionary policies of the Republicans and many Democrats. One could even argue that if Hussein didn't exist, someone like him would have to be created. Keep in mind that when Turkey invaded Cyprus, the United States didn't mumble opposition; when Israel invaded Lebanon and carried out military actions, the United States winked its approval.

The public is solemnly told that we may have to invade Kuwait to preserve the interests of "democracy"—never mind that we have no defense treaties with Kuwait, and that Kuwait has never been a democracy. Now we hear from the Bush administration that Iraq's capitulation from Kuwait wouldn't be enough; Hussein's military-industrial complex would also have to be destroyed in the bargain. In short, we have to destroy the country in order to save it. The same insane logic was responsible for Vietnam, and the thousands of American casualties.

The real question in this sorry tale is, "What happened to the liberals?" The Congressional Black Caucus, the conscience of the House of Representatives on budgetary policies, is curiously quiet. Neither the NAACP nor other civil rights groups have taken public stands against this lunacy in the desert sun. Liberal trade union leaders who should recognize their constituents' interests in moving toward economic conversion, have done nothing.

On other matters, the story is the same: liberals have gone under the political covers, capitulating to the right, waiting for the pro-war rhetoric to clear. Most of the liberal groups which vigorously opposed reactionary law professor Robert Bork three years ago for nomination to the Supreme Court did nothing to block conservative judge David Souter's appointment. The People for the American Way, the NAACP Legal Defense and Education Fund, and the American Civil Liberties Union, all stood on the sidelines.

Where are the liberals? The habits of 40 years of the Cold War, of apologizing for their opposition to unrestricted, rampant capitalism, their belief in a positive role for government, and their support for racial justice, are difficult to overcome. But without the courage of our convictions in challenging the inhumane, irrational and now pro-war policies of the Bush administration, we may give our opponents a new and undeserved lease on political life. Any political system which fails to provide real choices to its electorate is no democracy.

October 1990

Blacks and the Republicans:
A Marriage of Convenience?

Last month's controversy over the Bush administration's temporary decision to deny Federal funds to colleges awarding scholarships to minority students on the basis of race had an interesting secondary dimension. The bureaucrat announcing this new racist policy was an African American, Michael L. Williams, the Assistant Secretary for Civil Rights in the Department of Education. Williams justified the elimination of educational opportunity to thousands of Latino and black students by declaring that the policy paralleled other Bush administration positions on affirmative action and racial quotas. After Bush was forced to retreat, the hapless Williams was again pushed before television cameras to declare that the new policy would be replaced by yet another more moderate approach, which still rejected the use of racial quotas.

The white power system in this country has always used blacks to articulate discriminatory policies, to justify race and class exploitation. White America's "favorite Negro" a century ago was Booker T. Washington, the educator who defended the political disfranchisement of blacks and the expansion of racial segregation throughout society. A decade ago, Hoover Institution economist Thomas Sowell became prominent as the black apologist for Reaganism. The easiest way for blacks to become millionaires in this country is to publicly defend reactionary and racist policies. Williams is being used by a cynical system which perpetuates oppression on his own racial group.

But there's also evidence indicating that the connection between blacks and conservative Republicans is rooted in a curious convergence of interests. The Voting Rights Act of 1965 and subsequent Supreme Court decisions regarding minorities' voting rights have forced state legislatures to create districts in which blacks and Latinos comprise significant percentages. Today, about 80 white Democrats represent Congressional districts which are 30 percent black. Blacks and Mexican Americans represent the most dependable and reliable voting blocs that white Democrats have, especially in urban districts. So if Congressional district lines are redrawn to include greater numbers of black and hispanic candidates, other districts conversely will become "whiter" and "more affluent," a profile favoring Republicans.

This fact has not escaped conservative Republicans, who now display a strong interest in minority electoral participation. In a half-million dollar project, Benjamin L. Ginsberg, the chief counsel of the Republican National Committee, is collaborating with civil rights organizations to help them with technical assistance in proposing minority districts. Other Republican groups are offering Mexican Americans and blacks free computer time, legal assistance and tactical support.

Some statewide elections last year also indicate another kind of pragmatic cooperation between blacks and Republicans. In Illinois, Republican gubernatorial candidate Jim Edgar received public endorsements from several Chicago black leaders, largely due to the fact that his Democratic opponent had opposed the late mayor Harold Washington in his 1987 reelection campaign. About one-fifth of the black vote went to Edgar statewide, which provided the Republican with an unexpected margin of victory.

Black Americans understand that the Republican Party is clearly hostile to our interests. But politics makes strange bedfellows, and the refusal of white Democrats to take seriously the message of the Jesse Jackson challenge fragments the degree of partisanship and loyalty blacks have toward their party. Unless white Democrats really begin to champion blacks' interests, blacks in growing numbers will collaborate with Republicans at state and national levels.

January 1991

Why Blacks Oppose the War

Since January 15, this nation's white political leadership and a majority of the white public has gone crazy for war. The bulk of the white media accepts every pronouncement of the military as gospel. When U.S. bombers destroy a Baghdad air raid shelter, killing hundreds of innocent civilians, we are told approvingly that this was an act of "military necessity." When much of the world becomes outraged by the excessive force and slaughter initiated by indiscriminate bombing, our "leaders" reply smugly that all casualties are Saddam's fault. The wrongs committed by Iraq's invasion of Kuwait have been surpassed by the crimes committed by our own government against the people of Iraq. Yet millions of white Americans call for nothing less than Saddam's head as the price for peace.

Nevertheless, a substantial section of Americans have consistently opposed U.S. policy and militarism in the Persian Gulf. And the leading voices of this growing trend for peace are African Americans.

In opinion poll after poll, most blacks question the military and Bush administration polemics about the necessity of the Gulf conflict. A recent *New York Times*/CBS poll indicates that 63 percent of all whites and only 40 percent of all African Americans agreed with the statement that "the war to defeat Iraq is likely to be worth the loss of life and other costs." Forty-seven percent of all white Americans, but only 30 percent of all blacks polled, endorsed the statement that "a ground war to defeat Iraq would be worth the cost of losing thousands of American lives."

African-American politicians have been almost alone in Congress in condemning this conflict. Last month, only twelve House members refused to vote in favor of a resolution supporting the presence of American troops in the region and applauding President Bush for his "leadership as Commander-in-Chief." Ten of the twelve were African Americans. They recognized that this vote was actually a back-door endorsement of Bush's decision to initiate warfare. One African-American opponent of the war, Brooklyn Congressperson Major Owens, observed that his mail was approximately 100 to one against the conflict. Jesse Jackson also has condemned this war, speaking out at anti-war demonstrations. Jackson warned other Democratic Party leaders at a party conference last month that "bold leadership is not afraid to stand up for peace."

At the grassroots, thousands of black young people and activists have mobilized for peace. In New York, representatives from 19 different groups created the "African-American Coalition Against U.S. Intervention." At Howard University, undergraduates established the "Student Call Against the War," holding workshops and community-based activities. In Atlanta, the "Concerned Black Clergy" denounce U.S. policy in the Gulf, and called for a negotiated settlement of all issues. And in December, Eric Hayes, the president of the Black Student Association at Southern Illinois University, and a Marine reservist, was arrested after protesting against the war. Speaking for many young African Americans in the armed forces, Hayes declared that he refused to become "a pawn in America's power play for oil."

Blacks oppose this conflict because they remember the lessons of the Vietnam War. Many African Americans were assigned to combat units, and received much higher casualty rates than whites. Today, about 30 percent of the frontline troops in Saudi Arabia are African American. It is ironic that Bush believes that blacks are good enough to die for American and corporate interests abroad, but we aren't good enough for him to sign last year's Civil Rights Bill.

Blacks have a long tradition of opposing this country's military adventures abroad, especially in the third world. We know that the justification for wars against non-Europeans inevitably generates racism. And once unleashed, racism quickly targets people of color here at home. By opposing the war, black Americans stand up against racism and violence.

March 1991

Political Illiteracy

It has become fashionable to talk about the "new patriotism" across America, the wave of euphoria and self-congratulations which was generated by the American military's crushing of Iraq. George Bush tells us proudly that the "Vietnam Syndrome" of self-doubt and military malaise has been banished from the American conscience. Although most black Americans and other people of color still have criticisms of this most recent foreign adventure designed to distract us from our own very pressing problems at home, such as poverty, the urban crisis, and the savings and loan fiasco, the vast majority of whites have uncritically accepted the "new patriotism" rhetoric as reality. But viewed from a distance, the polemics of patriotism are grounded in political illiteracy, a perception of world affairs and public policies rooted in ignorance and a contempt for the interests of third world people.

Political illiteracy begins with the inability to define problems correctly. For example, Americans have been told that the war against Iraq was launched to protect critical oil supplies in the Mideast. The specter of 1973 gas lines, millions of lost jobs, and a crippling recession were conjured to add an element of panic within the calls for patriotism. Secretary of State James Baker summed up the American military response to Saddam Hussein in one simple word: "Jobs."

But in truth, no war for oil would have been necessary if the United States had a comprehensive national energy policy. Reducing oil consumption by one-eighth would eliminate the need for oil imports from Iraq and Kuwait combined. According to energy researchers Amory Lovins and L. Hunter Lovins, we currently have the technology to run the American economy on one-fifth the oil we are currently using.

Warfare is never explained to American people in practical, dollars and cents terms. If we increased fuel efficiency in our automobiles by nine miles per gallon per household, no Mideast oil would be necessary at all. When Americans fill up their cars at self-service gas stations, they don't compute the actual costs of gasoline, which should include the price of maintaining a massive military establishment to guarantee control of foreign oil resources. Computing military costs, Persian Gulf oil actually cost $100 per barrel. An M-1 tank travels at less than six-tenths of a mile per gallon.

Political illiteracy is an absence of critical knowledge about the major events, issues and personalities which comprise current affairs. Americans under the age of 30 are apathetic about politics, and have little comprehension of the world. According to a recent poll conducted by Times Mirror Center for the People and the Press, only one-third of all Americans aged 18 to 29 knew that the Soviet Union was encouraging the political reforms which have occurred in Eastern Europe during the Gorbachev period. Only 28 percent of all young respondents knew that the United States would give control of the Panama Canal to Panama, compared to 42 percent of those 50 and older. Most young people don't vote, don't read magazines or newspapers regularly for current events, and have difficulty placing countries on a world map. Is it any wonder that in the span of six months, the media and the Bush administration could manipulate the public from near total ignorance of Iraq, Kuwait and Saddam Hussein, to a war-frenzied desire to obliterate tens of thousands of innocent people.

When sound bites and symbolism replace intelligent analysis, when presidents brag openly that they will "kick ass," the possibilities for democratic discourse evaporate. Appealing to the worst instincts among us, political, corporate and media leaders rely on the "bread and circuses" technique to manipulate the public's perceptions. Unless we become more critical of what we are told, and demand greater diversity in political viewpoints, we also contribute to political illiteracy, and the bankruptcy of present policies.

April 1991

Chapter VII

Jesse Jackson,
The Election of 1988, and
the Bankruptcy
of American Politics

Race and Presidential Politics

Despite the unprecedented accomplishments of the Reverend Jesse Jackson in the 1988 Democratic primaries, there is substantial evidence indicating that millions of white voters rejected the progressive candidate largely on the grounds of race. According to the data compiled by University of California-Irvine professor Amihai Glazer, based on the results of 22 Democratic primaries, a 1 percent increase in the percentage of black voters in any state corresponded to a 1 percent decline in the fraction of white voters who supported Jackson in the state's Democratic primary. In other words, the more blacks who live, work and vote in any state, the fewer whites in that state who were willing to vote for Jackson.

For instance, Jackson received about one-third of the votes from whites in the state of Vermont, which has less than 1 percent black voting age population. Jesse obtained over 35 percent of the white vote in Oregon, which has a black population of 1 percent. In Ohio, however, where blacks represent about 12 percent of the electorate, Jackson's vote declined to about 17 percent among whites; in New York, with a black electorate of 14 percent, the white vote for Jackson dropped to 15 percent. In New Jersey, where one out of five Democratic voters is black, the white vote for Jackson declined to 13 percent.

In summary, the white electorate is far more "race conscious" in its electoral behavior than are blacks, who are accustomed to voting for white Democratic candidates year after year. Glazer suggests that covert racial bigotry is manifested within the political culture of whites to such an extent that it can be accurately measured: "you might get violent against Blacks...That's now not accepted, so one way of expressing these emotions is to vote against the candidate Blacks support."

The immediate consequences of Glazer's research have not escaped the considerations of the Bush and Dukakis campaigns. In 1984, Democratic presidential candidate Walter Mondale carried about 28 percent of the overall southern white vote; in states like Mississippi and Alabama, Mondale won less than 15 percent of the white vote. Symbolically, Mondale was perceived as the "Blacks' candidate," and given the degree of political weight accorded to racial considerations, the masses of whites threw their support behind Reagan, the candidate who symbolized "whites' interests."

Bush is trying to repeat Reagan's strategy, by building a white united front across the South. Tactically, he is trying to turn the Democrats' two-man ticket into a troika—Dukakis, Bentsen, and Jesse Jackson. In the conservative Democratic ethnic enclaves of the Midwest and East Coast, Bush is repeating the same tactic. In Chicago, he is aligned with the vicious racist, former Chicago Democratic boss "Fast Eddie" Vrdolyak; in Philadelphia, Bush is backed by former mayor and police chief Frank Rizzo. Bush has opposed vigorous enforcement of civil rights measures, and backed the destruction of the U.S. Civil Rights Commission. Perhaps more importantly, Bush's entire campaign has emphasized issues of concern which mobilize subliminal racial fears and anxieties among many whites. Without overt racist rhetoric, the Vice President is trying to create the impression that Dukakis is the "Blacks' candidate."

Dukakis could have seized the opportunity to build an effective anti-racist coalition, structured upon the successes of the Jackson campaign. He could have used the electoral forum as a bridge to link multi-cultural constituencies, while simultaneously condemning the Reagan-Bush record on civil rights and affirmative action. Instead, Dukakis has largely capitulated to the racist currents in white politics by accommodating to Bush's tactics. Last month, Dukakis gave a major speech at a county fair in Philadelphia, Mississippi, the site of the brutal murders of three civil rights workers in 1964. Dukakis not only failed to mention the executions, but neglected to outline his vision of a multiracial society founded on the principles of social justice for all. More recently, his campaign staff is reported to have ordered Jesse Jackson not to campaign in certain states, for fear of his sparking a white backlash against Dukakis. The only way to challenge racism is to attack it directly; in his failure to challenge racism in presidential politics, Dukakis is sowing the seeds of his own defeat.

September 1988

The Politics of Intolerance

Traditionally, presidential campaigns don't begin until after Labor Day. And the majority of American voters don't pay too much attention to the candidates until after the World Series begins. But 1988 seems to be an exception to the rule. Dukakis declined in the polls, in the wake of Bush's dishonest assault against his public record. The Republican mudslinging was persuasive, however, with many white working-class Democrats and southern whites who had voted for Reagan in 1984. Bush's advisers have a single-minded strategy to achieve victory for their candidate, a strategy which can be understood as the "politics of intolerance."

The politics of intolerance, first, creates political scapegoats who are supposedly responsible for all of the society's problems. For middle-to-lower-class whites who usually vote Democratic but who are fearful of crime, the Republican message is to conjure up the racist image of the black and hispanic criminal. For poor whites, create the target of the so-called lazy and shiftless welfare mother who buys choice steaks and drives a pink Cadillac. Pretend that the two million homeless Americans don't exist. Blame the Democrats for every environmental problem, from AIDS-infected needles on public beaches to toxic wastes in our drinking water, despite the reality that the Reaganites have done everything possible to relax if not entirely outlaw environmental protection laws. This is the politics of bigotry, ideological rigidity and national chauvinism. Many Democrats imitate the same right-wing strategy, but the Republican national ticket has elevated the politics of intolerance to a dangerous level, building upon the dogmatic and destructive foundations of Reaganism.

Another central feature of political intolerance is an unwillingness to accept the principle of pluralism and social diversity within the policies and practices of political organizations and institutions. It is a type of narrow political opportunism, which sacrifices the welfare of millions of minorities and those constituencies which experience systemic discrimination, intolerance, and economic oppression, for the benefit of the elitist few. Bush's entire public record is nothing but a monument to crass opportunism. For instance, years ago he supported the Voting Rights Act, but later opposed its extension. Bush pledges rhetorical support for the interests of white working women, but opposes federal funding for child care facilities, expanded job training programs and social services for women and their families.

The political offensive against blacks, hispanics, Native Americans, small farmers, women, workers, environmentalists, civil rights advocates, gays, lesbians, and other groups, assumes a distinct form in each case. Nevertheless, the general trend is toward greater authoritarian rhetoric, an anti-pluralistic and intolerant attitude toward the rights of minorities. When it is possible to blame feminists, people of color, union members, or other "greedy special interests" for one problem or another, without offering any serious or substantive evidence, a climate which promulgates public repression is inevitable. The scapegoating of minorities and oppressed social classes leads to the preemptive dismissal of their legitimate grievances; the intolerant politician loves to "blame the victim" for his/her exploitation, and argues that criminality among the poor is solely the product of individual choices, rather than largely the social and economic consequence of poverty, poor schools, social deprivation and class oppression. This elitist perspective reinforces the public's demand for the death penalty, the expansion of prison construction, and the passage of repressive legislation which could limit civil liberties.

The Bush-Quayle ticket is based on a narrow, right-wing agenda which reinforces the politics of intolerance, racial inequality, sexism, and social class divisiveness. If Bush manages to defeat Dukakis, Americans can anticipate a fundamental erosion of the democratic rights of minorities, and the acceleration of a racial backlash against affirmative action and civil rights.

September 1988

The Politics
of Race and Class Division:
An Analysis of the 1988
Presidential Campaign

The election of George Bush to the presidency in 1988 appears, in retrospect, to have been inevitable. Bush captured 40 out of 50 states, and received 54 percent of the popular vote. The country was at peace, and official unemployment rates stood at barely 5 percent. But a closer examination of the recent campaign provides a different interpretation. Bush did not "win" the election; it was "lost" by Dukakis and more specifically, by the ineptitude and failure of the national Democratic Party to counter the politics of class division and social intolerance promoted by Bush and the Republicans.

Dukakis never comprehended the significance of the primary campaign of Jesse Jackson. The black Democrat emerged as the leader of the party's progressive/left wing, winning more popular votes in the 1988 primaries than Walter Mondale achieved in 1984. Four million blacks voted for Jackson, but so did an additional three million Asians, hispanics and whites. A progressive challenge to "Reaganism" could expand the base of Democratic Party politics, which was the only viable recourse for Dukakis to challenge Bush.

Instead, Dukakis and his advisers closed the political door to the Left, and accepted the conventional wisdom that national elections are won by seizing the "center." In his acceptance address, the Massachusetts governor proclaimed that this election was not about "ideology, but competency." More significant was the selection of Texas Senator Lloyd Bentsen as Dukakis's running mate. The choice of the conservative Democrat was justified in historical terms, since no Democratic candidate had ever won the presidency in the twentieth century without carrying Texas. But Dukakis was making an ideological statement by tapping Bentsen. The ticket sent a message to the Party's power brokers, to Wall Street, and to executives in petrochemicals, construction, real estate, high tech, and other growth sectors of the economy. It proclaimed, in no uncertain terms, the return to power and prestige of the "Reagan Democrats" within the corridors of power. Dukakis was stating: "I'm a man you can do business with. I'm not an ideologue of the liberal left, but a pragmatist of the center." Minorities perceived that Dukakis was issuing a *racial* statement by selecting Bentsen: "Despite Jesse's unprecedented victories in the caucuses and primaries, the controls of the Party are firmly in the hands of the white male leaders right and center." Despite these maneuvers, Bentsen conspicuously failed to deliver his home state, and whites in the Sunbelt voted two-to-one against the Democratic ticket.

Bush's counter-strategy was simple: to emphasize simplistic, emotional issues in which the Democrats were vulnerable. Willie Horton became a household word, symbolic of Dukakis's so-called "weakness" on crime. The pledge of allegiance, abortion rights, and "reverse discrimination" became code phrases for the Republicans' "politics of intolerance," their unwillingness to accept the existence of social diversity and ideological pluralism within the policies and institutional practices of a democracy.

Bush's entire public record was nothing but a monument to this type of intolerance and opportunism. For example, Bush once backed the Equal Rights Amendment and favored women's right to a safe, legal abortion; now, he opposes the ERA, rejects federal funding for abortions in most instances, and denounces comparable worth on the job for women.

Bush's successful career is symbolic of the growth of intolerance generally within American political culture. Examples of political intolerance include the defeat of the ERA, the rejection of economic comparable worth; attacks against gay men and lesbians within the political system, such as the homophobic sodomy law which was passed by the Georgia state legislature; the suppression of the Native American rights movement, including the harassment of Indian protest leaders; and the continued offensive by the corporations and the Reagan-Bush administration against organized labor.

November 1988

The Demise of Liberalism

The recent victory of George Bush over Michael Dukakis in the 1988 presidential election has been interpreted as a victory of the Republican Party over the Democrats. The Republicans have won five out of six recent presidential elections, and seven out of ten national contests since 1952. But more accurately, Dukakis's defeat represents the political dead end of liberalism, and more generally, the public policies which most black Americans support.

The American political system is becoming increasingly stratified by race. In 1984, for example, 66 percent of all whites voted for the reelection of Ronald Reagan as president. This year, roughly 60 percent of all whites nationally, and approximately 70 percent of all southern whites, cast ballots for George Bush. In contrast, nearly nine out of ten black voters supported Dukakis. Since 1964, the black vote for the Democratic presidential candidate has averaged approximately 88 percent.

Dukakis recognized that he had to win a larger percentage of the middle-class white electorate than either Mondale or Carter if he was to have any hope of capturing the White House. To do this, Dukakis decided to distance himself from black issues in general, and from Jesse Jackson in particular. He didn't campaign in a black church or a major black community until only several weeks before the general election. He blandly assumed that blacks would vote for him, because with Bush as the alternative, they had nowhere else to go. But blacks were so disgruntled with the Massachusetts Democrat that thousands simply stayed home on election day, producing significantly lower turnout rates and damaging all other Democrats on the ballot.

Blacks distrusted Dukakis because, unlike Mondale, he lacked any political credentials in civil rights activism or support. But they also sensed a degree of political opportunism in his refusal to identify himself as a "liberal" throughout most of the presidential race. For the vast majority of black Americans, "liberalism" is a political term which has overwhelmingly positive connotations: the institutionalization of civil rights legislation, the creation of job training and social welfare programs, the implementation of affirmative action, minority economic set-asides, and public education programs.

Conversely, for the overwhelming majority of white middle class to upper-class voters, liberalism conjures up a motley collection of highly questionable social and economic policies. A wide variety of programs ranging from state prison furloughs to Aid to Families with Dependent Children are projected as somehow contributing to social permissiveness, social deviance, and even criminality. As real incomes for the middle class have shrunk during the past decade, the white middle class has become less benevolent towards the allocation of tax revenues to address the problems of the poor, the homeless, and the unemployed. Whites living in suburbia who earn $40,000 annually and more generally back the GOP because, in part, they consciously favor government policies which protect the material interests of the "haves" against the claims of the "have-nots." Liberalism was sacrificed upon the high altar of narrow self-interest. The clearest expression of this ideological rejection of liberalism is grounded in the popular calls for reduced federal and state taxes, the advocacy of the death penalty, stricter police enforcement, and deep cuts in social spending.

One of the reasons for the increasingly conservative perspective of both major parties is the subtle element of racism. Ever since the passage of the 1964 Civil Rights Act, broad sections of the white public have become convinced that the national leadership of the Democratic

Party has gone too far in guaranteeing blacks opportunities and rights, at the expense of the social mobility and
material welfare of the white majority.

Perhaps a generation ago, there existed a reservoir
of racial guilt toward the status of the Afro-American, the
product of several centuries of slavery, Jim Crow, and
socioeconomic discrimination. Many whites genuinely felt
uncomfortable when confronted with the brutal realities
of the ghetto, and earnestly favored policies which would
reduce overt racial prejudice. Legislation was passed to
extend basic constitutional rights to those who had been
unjustly denied them. But by the 1970s, as the power of
the black electorate increased, and as white males slipped
to a minority within the overall national labor force, a
sharp metamorphosis in public psychology occurred. Suddenly, there was the uneasy perception that "too much"
had been given to the Negro. Without resorting to the
racist vulgarities of a George Wallace, conservative politicians like Ronald Reagan cleverly tapped the new mood
of racial antipathy.

The recent rejection of liberalism at the polls is
therefore a reaction against people of color, an attempt to
check the advances of affirmative action and the broader
freedom struggle. The concepts of compensatory justice
and political compassion for the oppressed no longer have
mass support among the white middle class.

The consequences of the collapse of liberalism as a
dominant political philosophy within government will be
most painfully apparent within the economy. President-
elect Bush was never an advocate of Reagonomics prior to
1980; indeed, he denigrated the supply-side, lower tax
dogmas as "voodoo economics." Yet throughout the 1988
campaign, Bush proclaimed: "Read my lips: no new taxes."
It was good political rhetoric, but very poor economic
policy, considering the multi-billion dollar deficits which
the federal government hemorrhages annually. Despite
the appointment of non-ideologues to important economic

policy positions, notably Richard G. Darman as director of the Office of Management and Budget, the markets doubt that Bush will be able to extricate himself from his irrational campaign promises.

The Federal Reserve Board will move toward tighter monetary policies to defend the value of the dollar abroad. This will contribute to higher interest and inflation rates. Cutbacks in production could trigger a chain reaction, culminating in a severe recession within 12 to 15 months. The scenario above points to the necessity to reduce federal expenditures, such as cutting the bloated Pentagon budget. But the logic of political conservatism will mean balancing the budget on the backs of those who can least afford austerity. That means even deeper cuts in social welfare, public housing, education and social programs which address the needs of minorities, working people and the poor. Despite Bush's declaration that he wants to become known as the "Education President," his economic agenda threatens to erode any possibility of advances in public education. The prospects for job training programs targeting the hardcore unemployed will become even bleaker in the 1990s.

December 1988

Toward
a Rainbow Government

The Rainbow Coalition which supported Jesse Jackson's presidential campaigns in 1984 and 1988 must move to the next logical stage of development in the struggle for power. We need to rethink our political strategy, and develop more effective methods to advance our agenda.

Part of the problem of black and progressive politics in recent years has been that too much emphasis has been placed on presidential politics. To be sure, the presidency is a powerful position, dominating the government's agenda and determining the composition of the Supreme Court and the federal bureaucracy. By contesting the Democratic Party's presidential nomination in 1984 and 1988, Jackson elevated the progressive agenda on foreign and domestic policies, while acting as an invaluable counterweight to the Democrats' ideological stampede to the right. But a rerun of this strategy which places too much of our energies and resources in the presidential primaries in 1992 could be counterproductive.

We need to take a serious look at the strengths, contradictions, and possibilities of America's electoral system, and the next necessary steps for maximizing progressive empowerment. At the federal level, it is difficult for progressives to mount serious challenges to incumbents in either party. The turnover rate of the House of Representatives who have been reelected at least one time is much lower than the turnover rate of the Soviet Union's Communist Party Central Committee. Similarly, despite the victories in presidential primaries and caucuses by Jackson last year, it is highly unlikely that anyone with Rainbow Coalition-type politics would emerge with the

Democratic presidential nomination before the year 1996. One probable electoral scenario three years from now will be the coalition of white conservative and centrist Democrats behind a "great white hope," possibly Virginia Senator Chuck Robb, New Jersey Senator Bill Bradley, or even ex-vice presidential hopeful Lloyd Bentsen. The "trade-off" to the party's liberal wing could be the selection of an hispanic or African-American vice presidential running mate, such as Congressperson Bill Gray of Philadelphia. The party bosses will leave no stones unturned in order to defeat Jesse Jackson, no matter how "reasonable" or "moderate" he becomes.

White conservative Democrats continue to look for a scapegoat to explain the reason for their defeat in five of the six most recent presidential races. Jackson's trying to repackage himself as a more credible or "responsible" factor within the party. But no amount of repositioning will permit Jackson or anyone else with progressive left politics, such as Texas's Jim Hightower or California Congressperson Ron Dellums, to assume the mantle of presidential leadership. This opposition has nothing to do with personality, but with power and ideology. What the Rainbow represents is simply too threatening to the class interests which dominate the party. Moreover, given the conservative electoral behavior of the bulk of the white upper-to-middle-classes, the Republicans will have a tremendous advantage over any Democrat in the next two presidential general elections.

But if we shift the focus to local electoral politics, a more optimistic picture emerges for progressives. There are a total of 504,404 elective offices in the United States. This is an increase for more than 14,000 public offices since 1977. Most of these offices are held by township officials, town clerks, members of school boards, and municipal officials. In many states, it takes relatively little money or organization to run successfully for a position as state representative, or for a town's school board. These positions permit people who have an interest in political work to gain experience and to acquire necessary leadership skills to serve their constituencies. Progressives must think globally, but act locally. We need to reemphasize the electoral struggle for empowerment at the neighborhood, school district, and community level. Keep in mind that although African Americans represent 12.5 percent of the population, they hold only 3.3 percent of municipal positions; they account for only 2.6 percent of the county officials, 2.4 percent of all school district office holders, 0.6 percent of the special district officials and only 0.4 percent in town offices. Women represent about 26.5 percent of school board members, and only 18.5 percent of municipal officials. Only 1 percent of all office holders are Latinos, despite an hispanic population of more than 7 percent. In short, blacks, hispanics and women remain grossly under-represented within the electoral arena.

A political vehicle outside of the Democratic Party is needed to engage in successful electoral competition. In some districts, progressives may be able to "take over" the Democratic organization and press forward with an effective, Rainbow agenda. But in most cases, the Democratic regulars will attempt to block and frustrate the progressive forces. What's required is a network or organization of activists who have personal histories of struggle inside civil rights, feminist, labor, peace movement, gay rights, and community-based formations. This network, if connected with the Rainbow, must have a system of democratic accountability. The national leadership or spokespersons must be directly elected and accountable to the membership. The struggle for democratic leadership must be waged inside the Rainbow. Such a force could help to mobilize students on college campuses, who are now searching for leadership in their struggles against tuition hikes, racism and sexism within the curriculum and cutbacks in minority recruitment. It could link activists inside the labor movement who are struggling against

plant shutdowns and union concessions to the corporations. But to do so, it must develop a viable national
presence and organizational structure. At minimum, this
means the funding of a national, monthly newspaper,
which highlights the activism of local groups. Regional
offices are needed, not simply a room with a telephone,
but a regular meeting place for progressives. We need a
national theoretical journal which critiques the recent
lessons of political struggles, and especially the successes
and failures of the Rainbow. But most importantly, we
need field organizers, itinerant activists going from city
to city, distributing literature and linking the various
constituencies into a viable, national movement.

If those who supported Jesse Jackson last year are
truly committed to a progressive vision of democracy, we
must build a political movement and an organizational
capability which goes far beyond the Democratic Party.
The goal must be a national Rainbow government by the
year 2000.

February 1989

Why the Rainbow Coalition Has Failed

The most progressive political leader at the national level for the past decade has been Jesse Jackson. Yet many observers of Jackson's Rainbow Coalition politics are now wondering whether the historical opportunity has been lost for creating a more progressive alternative in politics.

When Jackson first ran for the presidency, few seriously believed that he would achieve the Democratic Party's nomination. His campaign was a social protest movement which used the Democratic primaries to increase black voter turnout and to reinforce the power of the liberal-left wing of the Democratic Party. By 1988, Jackson had shifted closer to the center, and permitted black officials who had campaigned vigorously against him four years before to dominate municipal and statewide mobilizations.

The Rainbow failed to develop a coherent national apparatus, with a national newspaper, regional political organizers, and trained cadre on campuses and in communities. Local activists drawn into the Jackson campaigns weren't encouraged to develop autonomous coalitions which were independent of the national electoral effort. Jackson's frenetic, larger-than-life personality and his chaotic organizational style, consisting of a coterie of loyalists who rarely disagree with the boss, works against genuinely democratic decisionmaking.

Part of the problem was the bitterly ironic relationship which developed unexpectedly between Jackson and the newly prominent black politicians like Doug Wilder. Jackson's Rainbow had been responsible for elevating black politics to the national arena, illustrating that a black candidate could compete successfully, winning presidential caucuses and elections in states without sizeable minority groups. It was Jackson, not David Dinkins, who proved that a black candidate for high office could win a plurality of votes against more conservative, white candidates in New York City. Jackson's candidacy forced the Democratic Party to liberalize its posture towards women and minority candidates.

Jackson's candidacies opened the political space for black officials seeking statewide and mayoral positions, although running challenges which were more conservative than Jackson's. Doug Wilder's victory as Virginia's governor was based partially on Jackson's strategy, holding on to the black vote while winning about one third of all whites' votes. But his political program was clearly more conservative than Jackson's. Once elected, Wilder lost little time endorsing centrist policy positions and repudiating liberal activism representing the party's left wing. Andrew Young's gubernatorial campaign in Georgia, in which he has endorsed the death penalty, faithfully follows the Wilder model, not Jackson's. Jackson's continuing flirtation with presidential politics, and the reason for his refusal to run against Marion Barry in the District of Columbia's mayoral race, is partially due to his fear that Wilder is being groomed to surpass him.

Complicating matters is Jackson's tense and ambiguous relationship with Louis Farrakhan. Jackson has known Farrakhan intimately for more than a quarter century; Chicago was the political base for both men. In 1984, especially in the early stages of the Democratic primaries, Jackson relied heavily on the Nation of Islam for security. Insiders within the Jackson inner circle state candidly that Jackson is literally afraid of alienating Farrakhan personally or his black nationalist constituency. Farrakhan has developed an extremely loyal cadre which expounds a conservative version of racial separatism and entrepreneurialism. Jackson fears a split with the nationalists which would repeat the hostilities which separated Martin Luther King from Malcolm X a generation ago. He is personally repulsed by the anti-Semitism and authoritarian elements of the Nation of Islam's ideology, yet feels constrained from denouncing this movement for fear of turning this militant sect against him.

Thus a stalemate exists in black electoral politics, in which Rainbow activism has reached a dead end, and black centrist politicians are beginning to take decisive initiatives. The failure here is not simply tactical, but strategic. Jackson's political perspective is still frozen in the era of the civil rights movement of the 1960s. His basic instincts are to pressure the Democratic Party to the left, rather than to map a strategy to change the nature of the political rules.

The idea of moving the Democratic Party to the left is an illusion plaguing civil rights leaders and black politicians for several generations. We really don't have two political parties, just one, the "Republicrats," both of which are controlled by corporate and upper class interest.

For the Rainbow to be relevant again, activists must revive the traditions and tactics of non-electoral political struggle. This means the creation of new institutions of resistance. For example, "freedom schools," open multiracial academies held during late afternoons and on weekends for secondary school and college students, could offer a public protest curriculum. Learning how to organize street demonstrations, selective buying campaigns, civil disobedience, and reading about the personalities and history of American protest, would help to revive the radical consciousness of this generation of youth.

Instead of worrying about whether Jackson will contest the Democratic Party's presidential nomination in 1992, progressives should refocus our electoral efforts on other priorities. More resources must be devoted to increasing the size of the electorate. The National Voter

Registration Act, passed last February in the House, should be a major legislative priority for civil rights groups. The bill would automatically update voters' rolls with information provided from updated applications for drivers' licenses and renewals and reports of address changes given to motor vehicle departments. Since non-voters are disproportionally nonwhite, poor, unemployed and/or working-class women, any significant increase from this constituency could shift the electoral results leftward, regardless of the individual candidates running for public office. We must pursue innovative strategies to transform the system, fulfilling the Rainbow's promise.

June 1990

Chapter VIII

Black Protest and Empowerment

Wanted: An Agenda
for Black Empowerment

A half century ago, the black community's leaders bought into a political strategy of reliance and dependency upon the Democratic Party in national elections. The goal was to increase our collective power within the electoral system, and to eradicate Jim Crow segregation. Unquestionably, for a time, this single-party approach yielded substantial benefits. Civil rights legislation, economic and social welfare programs, minority set-asides, and affirmative action were largely byproducts of this coalition approach which gave millions of black votes to white Democrats.

But as last year's presidential elections only reconfirm, the old liberal coalition has become permanently unglued. The leadership of the Democratic Party is rapidly moving rightward on questions of race and economic justice. More importantly, apparently Democratic presidential candidates lack the capacity to win national elections against the Republicans, despite the party's continued domination in the Congress. Since 1969, Democrats have controlled the executive branch of the federal government for only four years. Since the vast majority of black administrators and would-be public officials are Democrats, this has meant that they are generally shut out of decision-making posts within government. Because the civil rights organizations are heavily linked, politically and financially, to traditionally Democratic constituencies, their political clout in the Reagan administration was virtually nonexistent.

Facing the apparent permanency of the white electorate's conservatism, a number of black political leaders and political commentators are now suggesting that the solution to the dilemma of black powerlessness within the electoral arena can be gained by the move to Republicanism. Roy Innis, head of CORE, suggested recently the need to cultivate a bipartisan approach to electoral politics. For different reasons and employing a different approach, Tony Brown takes basically the same position. A larger number of entrepreneurially-inclined, younger African Americans have already joined the GOP, attempting to reap the potential benefits of opportunism and tokenism. Most of the new black Republicans do not support Reagan and Bush for ideological reasons. Unlike the black neoconservatives Thomas Sowell and Glen Loury, they have no ideological commitment to laissez-faire economics or an avowed hatred of affirmative action.

The new black Republicans simply recognize that the GOP is basically a white party, which for purposes of political appearance must nurture and promote a tiny number of middle-class blacks. It's no longer acceptable in American political culture to appear to be vulgarly racist, so a certain number of blacks provide a proper cover to justify repressive policies against the black community as a whole. Racism may underscore Bush's entire social and economic agenda, but the new administration must nevertheless go through the motions of appointing a token number of African Americans, mostly in symbolic positions. These few nonwhites who participate at the doors of the corridors of power are well-rewarded.

But the solution to the question of black powerlessness is not to be found by leaping from the political frying pan into the fire. The Republican Party is dominated by the most conservative and reactionary constituencies in white corporate America; the entire leadership of the Republican party throughout the South is largely the old Dixiecrat, segregationist reactionaries who opposed Dr. King and the civil rights movement. We can only begin to address our own political dilemma by establishing two things: an independent, aggressive political organization which can articulate the legitimate grievances of black working people and advance our own public policy agenda; and by setting strategic goals for the achievement of that agenda, no matter who occupies the White House.

An agenda for black empowerment must tackle the long-term issues which every black community across this nation must address: hunger, poverty, inadequate housing, poor public health care, the lack of economic self-sufficiency and development, affirmative action. We need to develop a better strategic relationship with that section of the hispanic community, the Puerto Ricans and Mexican Americans, who share a number of common economic and social problems with us. But most importantly, we must develop a political vehicle and a coherent agenda which advocates our interests without reservations or qualifications. Neither the Democrats nor the Republicans can liberate us. We must do so ourselves.

January 1989

How Black Power
was Lost in Chicago

The victory of State's Attorney Richard Daley over black incumbent Eugene Sawyer for the Democratic nomination in Chicago's mayoral primary was not unexpected. Sawyer was a dull, uninspiring candidate, and had no coherent or progressive program to address the city's problems in housing, health care, economic development or education. But the margin of his defeat by Daley, a massive 101,000 vote mandate, is indicative of the broader political dilemma for black politics throughout the country. Only six years ago, Congressperson Harold Washington swept to victory in Chicago's Democratic primary and general election, becoming the city's first mayor to represent an insurgent coalition of blacks, hispanics, and progressive elements of labor and the liberal white constituencies of the city's lakefront. Now, the immediate question is: How was black and progressive power lost in Chicago?

When Washington became mayor, the majority of black elected officials, leading clergymen and many black entrepreneurs had opposed his initial candidacy. They believed incorrectly that it was premature to talk about black, brown and progressive electoral power in Chicago. Washington himself was unsure whether to run, and it took a massive voter registration campaign in 1982 to make the mayoral race possible. However, Washington was not vindictive in victory. He did not lead a campaign to oust Congressperson Cardiss Collins from her House seat, despite her endorsement of Washington's opponent, Mayor Jane Byrne, in 1983. He permitted machine hacks from the Puerto Rican, Mexican-American and African-American communities to join his administration, regard-

185

less of their past political records of compromise and accommodation. Washington believed correctly that by the pressure from the masses of nonwhite and progressive voters from below, such politicians could be "remade" or reformed. This had been his own political trajectory and experience after his decisive break from the old Daley machine in the early 1970s.

When Washington was reelected in 1987, he failed to purge those elements within his coalition who were ideologically conservative, closest to the downtown business interests. He also permitted blacks who had openly campaigned against him to retain their ward seats unchallenged. But the major error committed by Washington was the failure to groom a logical political successor, who would stand for his progressive, anti-machine principles. Perhaps Washington felt that he would actually be mayor for another twenty years, despite his weight problem, chain-smoking, and generally bad personal health. For whatever reason, when the mayor died of a heart attack, no one in his own coalition was prepared to move forward with a plan to maintain the essential coalition between blacks, hispanics, and liberal whites which produced Washington's electoral victories.

The racist political machine of Edward Burke and Company, the heirs to the Daley organization, recognized one thing immediately: they could not elevate a white political leader into the mayor's seat in the aftermath of Washington's death. This was impossible, given the majority held by the Washington coalition in the City Council. They had to split their opponents, selecting the weakest, most vacillating black leader who was willing to betray the grassroots struggle for democracy. Sawyer was more than willing to play the puppet's role, despite the fact that the majority of Washington's forces favored Alderman Timothy Evans to become mayor. With white conservative support, Sawyer became mayor in a raucous City Council session besieged by angry black and hispanic demonstrators. Daley's victory was partially won the night Sawyer became mayor.

Sawyer's subsequent record as mayor could be best described as "transitional," as the white Democratic Machine and local corporate establishment simply marked time before the reins of power would be turned over to them. Sawyer seemingly made decisions which would facilitate the renaissance of white power. He failed to establish a political organization which could reach voters in the projects and community centers. He had no political agenda and worse, apparently no progressive vision which built upon the legacy of the late mayor Harold Washington. Sawyer went after official endorsements and television advertisements, without trying to solicit the support of ordinary working-class voters.

But Daley had other advantages as well. He was inarticulate and not too bright, to be sure. But his father had been boss of the city for more than two decades. The junior Daley had run in city and county-wide elections seven times since 1980, whereas Sawyer had never run for public office outside of the 6th Ward. White conservative and liberal would-be challengers, such as 14th Ward Alderman Edward Burke, former Chicago Park District Superintendent Edmund Kelly and 5th Ward Alderman Lawrence Bloom, dropped out or stepped aside, and erratic demagogue "Fast Eddie" Vrdolyak ran a successful write-in campaign for the Republican mayoral nomination. Daley also was successful in raising funds, spending approximately $1.8 million on media alone. With sufficient fiscal resources, plus the advantage of a one-on-one race against an unpopular black mayor, Daley should have trounced Sawyer.

Wisely, Daley also ran a campaign which minimized racial polemics. Although Daley had been defeated by Washington in the 1983 Democratic mayoral primary, coming in a poor third behind incumbent mayor Jane Byrne, he distanced himself from the acrimonious and confrontational style of Vrdolyak. Speaking in black churches just before election day, Daley tried to blur the distinction between progressive and reactionary politics by focusing on elements of style. "Harold Washington was a strong mayor who believed in open government and who talked about fairness," Daley declared. Daley applauded the Washington legacy, stating only that he had "a different style, a different management style" from his former opponent. Daley's only major gaffe was using the phrase "white mayor" at an appearance before an all-white crowd, in an effort to whip up a decent turnout among race-conscious voters.

There were also defections from the original Washington coalition to Daley. Many lakefront white liberals who had endorsed Washington returned to the fold by joining Daley. Joan Peters, a former administrator under Jimmy Carter and a supporter of Washington, backed Daley. One group of Jewish liberals, represented by a formation called the Jewish Committee for Responsible Government, refused to support Sawyer because of the mayor's "inability to act firmly and decisively in the face of overt anti-Semitism." The major defection occurred in the Latino community, as 26th Ward Alderman Luis Gutierrez campaigned extensively for Daley. Back in 1987, Washington carried the 26th Ward, which has thousands of hispanic voters, by a 4,300-vote margin over Jane Byrne. In this election, Daley defeated Sawyer by 4,300 votes in the 26th Ward. In the middle-class lakefront 49th Ward, Washington had defeated Byrne by a narrow 400-vote margin; two years later, Daley defeated Sawyer in the same ward by 3,600 votes. Citywide, Sawyer won less than 8 percent of the white vote.

Embittered and disappointed, Sawyer now refuses to endorse Tim Evans's independent race for mayor against Daley in the general election. Sawyer thus places his own frustrated ambitions above the fundamental interests of the black community, preferring to return the political establishment to the corrupt status quo. If black and progressive power is lost in Chicago as it was in Cleveland two decades ago with the demise of the administration of former mayor Carl Stokes, there is a very real possibility that no black or Latino mayor could emerge in that city for another ten years or more.

But there is one additional shadow cast by the fiasco of fragmented black power in Chicago. Jesse Jackson and his former campaign manager Ron Brown, now the Chairperson of the Democratic National Committee, played curious roles in the campaign. After some moments of uncertainty, Jackson embraced Sawyer for reelection, calling upon blacks to "Keep the Keys" to City Hall. Operation PUSH president Rev. Willie Barrow and other black leaders who had been close to Jackson over the years were key Sawyer supporters.

With Daley's victory, however, Brown pledged his "full support to the election of a Democratic mayor of the City of Chicago … The emphasis for all Democrats must now be on unity and conciliation." Jackson challenged the party hierarchy by announcing his support for Evans's insurgent campaign in the general election. If Evans has any chance for victory, he must rebuild the Washington progressive coalition, and Jackson must assume a critical role in this process without overshadowing the local candidate.

But is Jackson actually committed to the progressive, grassroots politics of a Harold Washington? At the most recent national meeting of the leaders of the Rainbow Coalition, Jackson's allies passed new requirements which would permit the appointment of state chairs, rather than their democratic election. If progressive politics means anything, it must mean mass participation and activism from below, which empowers working-class and low-income people. Black and progressive power was lost in Chicago because Sawyer failed to understand this fundamental reality.

March 1989

The African-American Summit: An Assessment

The African-American Summit held in New Orleans on April 21-23 was promoted as the most important gathering of black leaders and activists since the historic black political convention of March 1972, held in Gary, Indiana. The Gary Convention represented a highwater mark of black activism. The New Orleans Summit tried to recapture the political initiative for the black community, undermined for years by Reaganism, political conservatism and economic reaction. But despite its ability to attract over 1,200 delegates, observers and media representatives during a three-day period, it failed to propose a concrete strategy which could unite most black working people behind a progressive agenda.

The African-American Summit's political godfather was former Gary, Indiana mayor Richard Hatcher. One of the principal convenors of the earlier Gary Convention, Hatcher exercised considerable political clout during the Carter Administration. Despite his defeat for reelection as Gary's mayor, he has remained a power within black politics, partially due to his close personal relationship with Jesse Jackson. Following Bush's victory last November, Hatcher concluded that a major conference was needed, bringing together the major political figures in the African-American community. Of critical assistance to Hatcher's plans were the contributions of Ronald Walters, Howard University political scientist and Jackson advisor. To solicit the support of conservative blacks, Hatcher recruited Republican leader Gloria Toote to assist him.

The call for the Summit issued by Hatcher evoked the historical tradition of black struggle since the very first black political convention held in 1830. "This Summit would not be possible were it not for the landmark meetings of the past, those gatherings where agendas were set, strategies were fixed, the African-American cause advanced," Hatcher declared. The Summit would be "open to all African Americans of every political persuasion, religious organization, and all economic levels, ages, philosophies and walks of life." In short, the "greater our diversity at this summit," Hatcher stated, "the stronger the mandate which emerges."

Walters was more specific than Hatcher in outlining the expectations and goals of the proposed gathering. "We meet in order to regain the forward momentum in our movement," Walters stated before the Summit. "We have not done enough to stop both major parties from taking our vote for granted, to make our leadership more responsive....(We need) to develop a more powerful leadership strategy." Hatcher served as the Summit's chairperson, with honorary chairs extended to traditional civil rights leaders, such as NAACP secretary Ben Hooks, Urban League director John Jacob, SCLC leader Joseph Lowery, Jesse Jackson and Coretta Scott King. But the actual work in mobilizing the conference rested with the steering committee, whose members included Walters, Toote, progressive state legislators Dave Richardson of Pennsylvania and Maxine Waters of California, and Romona H. Edelin, President of the National Urban Coalition.

The conference workshops covered a variety of themes—education, civil rights, criminal justice, economic development, health care, blacks and the labor movement. Theoretically, statements from the workshops would be consolidated into a statement of African-American policy priorities, "in an effort to challenge government, Congress and the philanthropic community," according to Walters. To solicit a popular response to the Summit, the organizers relied upon Jesse Jackson's formidable powers of political persuasion. "This conference was devised as a free marketplace of ideas," Jackson declared.

"If we ever as a family needed to come together, we certainly need to come together now. We must seek common ground."

Given the cast of political characters, it was predictable that trouble would first surface from the far right. When Walters and other more liberal members of the Steering Committee identified several participants with controversial views on the left, such as Angela Davis and Amiri Baraka, many black Republicans threatened to walk out. When Louis Farrakhan's name was raised as a possible major speaker, the black Republicans and many Democrats nearly bolted. "Ideological diversity" to them meant the inclusion of black Reaganites and traditional liberals, but not black nationalists, socialists or non-partisan independents. The liberals and progressives on the steering committee won the argument for free speech, but with limitations. Davis was allowed to speak at a workshop, but not at a large plenary session. Lenora Fulani, the independent presidential candidate of the New Alliance Party, was also relegated to a workshop. Farrakhan was permitted to speak at a plenary, but on Sunday morning at nine a.m., not a convenient time. Farrakhan's marginal presence was still enough to frighten away some black conservatives, and possibly some civil rights leaders. Neither Hooks nor Jacob were in attendance, despite their endorsements of the Summit.

The Summit experienced some technical and logistical problems which inevitably occur at mass meetings. But beyond the level of minor disorganization was a more serious political contradiction between local black progressives vs. Summit leaders and their chief local sponsor, New Orleans mayor Sidney J. Barthelemy. The black activists charged the Summit with violating its own principles by charging $25 admission fees for observers, and $15 for students. Voting delegates had to pay even more. A small but spirited protest was sparked outside the doors of the conference. Finally, low-income people and youth were permitted to enter plenary sessions without charge. A few paying delegates witnessing the controversy complained that poor people who couldn't afford $25 apiece "shouldn't be allowed" into the Summit. This unreported dispute reveals in partial form the class divisions within the black community, a growing schism in which a significant sector of the black middle class has distanced itself politically and socially from the masses of our people. The common struggle for democratic rights and against racism obscures these class divisions, but they threaten to undermine any possibility of black unity inside political organizations.

The chief shortcoming of the Summit was its failure to call for operational unity across organizational and ideological lines. Many delegates assumed that because all participants were African Americans, we could shed partisan labels, ideologies and political views for the sake of unity. Perhaps this approach might work in some political utopia, but in the real world it is a recipe for disaster. Principled, operational unity does not mean that people obscure their differences. They must identify areas of commonality in which joint activities are in their respective interests.

At the major plenary session on politics, in which I participated, strikingly different and conflicting perspectives were advanced. Faye Williams, civil rights lawyer and former Congressional candidate in Louisiana, brought the audience to its feet with the assertion: "White people cannot tell us who our leaders will be...we must groom our people early and support them to run for office." No one could disagree, but Williams didn't outline a strategy for political activity. Similarly, former Gary, Indiana mayor Richard Hatcher informed the audience, "We get the kinds of politicians we deserve...if you're in public office, and you do what you feel like doing, you will not serve your constituency." Hatcher suggested that the quality of black elected officials could improve if "a national African American lobby" and public policy center on black politics were created "to protect our interests." But nothing in Hatcher's presentation represented a critique of the strengths and weaknesses of black politics during the post-civil rights era.

The most creative and manipulative presentation was given by black Republican leader Gloria Toote. Recognizing that the audience would be heavily oriented toward black nationalism, Toote came prepared, wearing a type of dashiki and quoting Malcolm X and W.E.B. Du Bois throughout her speech. The black adviser to Reagan and Bush declared: "What strategy should we adopt to maximize power in the 1990s? We need a strategy which will insure our survival. We have no permanent friends, no permanent enemies, only permanent interests." Although Toote defended her allegiance to the Republican Party, she hinted that part of the strategy of empowerment could involve a third party. Upon occasion, "we must seek power by taking risks…and explore Third Party options." Toote consciously mimicked Malcolm X by observing: "We must cease to place party labels above our racial interests."

Toote's strategy was transparent. The record of the Reagan-Bush administrations on civil rights and socioeconomic problems of African Americans is disastrous. Without discussing Bush's pandering to racism in last year's campaign, Toote attempts to advance a neo-Booker T. Washington economic program and a dependency upon conservative Republicans by using the rhetoric of Malcolm, Garvey, and Adam Clayton Powell.

An effective strategy for black empowerment must begin by recognizing the limitations of the electoral system in addressing our basic problems. We frequently think of power as purely an electoral process. But there is also power when oppressed people acquire a sense of cultural integrity and an appreciation of their political heritage of resistance. There is power when we mobilize our collective resources in the media, educational institutions, housing, health care and economic development to address issues. There is power when black people and other oppressed constituencies mobilize a march or street demonstration, when we use a boycott or picket line to realize our immediate objectives.

A strategy for African-American empowerment means that black politicians must be held more closely accountable to the interests of black people. Power implies the ability to reward and punish friends and enemies alike. Can blacks continue to afford to conduct voter registration and education campaigns, and then do nothing to check the voting behavior of our elected officials? Accountability must be measured objectively according to a list of policy priorities, and not be determined by political rhetoric at election time. One method to consider could be the creation of "people power" assemblies: popular, local conventions open to the general black public. Politicians of both major parties would be evaluated and ranked according to their legislative or executive records, and their responses on specific policy questions. Neither the Democratic nor the Republican Party can be expected to provide this level of direct accountability.

African-American empowerment must mean that all major political groups must encourage the democratic exchange of views, and the full participation of all black people in the decision-making process—including the unemployed, the homeless, elderly, youth and students, working women, and others who lacked the funds to travel to New Orleans or to pay the $25 registration fee. Empowerment also means that public forums and conventions must be accessible and affordable to the black masses. There exists no black so-called middle-class road to freedom which detours or ignores the dire situation of the black poor, working class, and the unemployed.

Empowerment should also connote the establishment of both a program and a strategy for progressive politics. At New Orleans, delegates adopted a fairly good program which covered many different issues. But a program is only a road map for where a constituency intends to go; what's missing is a strategy which guides the realization of that program. It would be as if we constructed a highly accurate compass, indicating where we needed to move, but lacked a vehicle to get us to that place. The strategies of the civil rights period, the alliances with Democrats and corporate liberals, are no longer relevant. We live in a new historical period, requiring leaders with imagination and vision to challenge the status quo.

May 1989

Do Blacks Deserve Reparations?

One central principle of international law is that people who have been the victims of systemic oppression over a period of time have the right to demand material compensation to redress their grievances. West Germany extended compensation to the state of Israel for the crimes committed against the Jewish people by the regime of Adolph Hitler. Thousands of Japanese Americans were unjustly interned in prison camps by the United States during World War II, and have recently won the right to demand compensation.

For many years, African Americans have argued that some type of economic compensation should be extended to blacks for the centuries of institutional racism and class exploitation. Seven decades ago, writer Arthur Anderson called for the creation of an all-black state termed "Moderna," and demanded that the American government provide reparations totalling $600 million. In the 1960s, many Black Power advocates agitated for compensation from white religious organizations and the government. Today, the call for reparations has acquired new impetus by the actions of Massachusetts State Senator Bill Owens. Owens has introduced Senate Bill 1621, calling upon the state "to provide for the payment of reparations for slavery, the slave trade and invidious discrimination against the people of African descent born or residing in the United States of America." The bill would require Massachusetts to "establish an African reparations commission which shall negotiate with legitimate representation of African descendants born in the United States for the payment of reparations."

Owens's call for reparations has sparked a national debate among blacks. In his view, the call for reparations "is not new. It has been a political issue since the Reconstruction period following the Civil War, when we were promised 40 acres and a mule as a form of compensation for the free labor that helped to build this country." In short, blacks have been the victims of super-exploitation, and compensation is only fair and just.

The Detroit City Council concurs with Owens, and recently approved a proposal for Congress to pay black Americans $40 billion in an education fund. Economist Julianne Malveaux also declares: "African Americans are the only people who came to the USA in chains. Although our labor laid the foundation for this country's infrastructure, we were never paid wages for that labor."

But some blacks have gone to unusual lengths to deplore the talk about reparations. Newspaper columnist Lawrence Wade pleased millions of conservative whites by declaring: "The USA owes this black man nothing." The historical clock which kept time on black oppression had no meaning for Wade. "How many bones of my ancestors who fought their enslavement lie along the ocean floor?" Wade asked. "What good for me now to count them? Isn't it time we put this race foolishness behind us?"

Wade's intellectual poverty is only overshadowed by his contempt for the reality of black history. How many Jewish Americans would say, "Let's forget about the Holocaust, and anti-Semitism"? How many American Indians would forget the terrible genocide their people have suffered? Through the periods of slavery, Jim Crow segregation, and urban ghettoization, African-American people have been underpaid for equal work, the last hired and the first fired. We own no huge corporations, and the total net assets of all black-owned corporations are smaller than a few multinationals. We have the right to demand economic and social compensation until equality is a reality.

June 1989

C.L.R. James:
A Black Political Giant

Earlier this month, in London, C.L.R. James died at the age of 88. Not widely known in the United States, James nevertheless is one of the most important black political theorists and scholars of the twentieth century.

Born in Trinidad, James travelled to England in the early 1930s and quickly became involved in radical politics. Collaborating with fellow Trinidadian George Padmore and artist/activist Paul Robeson, James helped to spark a growing movement for Pan-Africanism and the independence of Africa and the Caribbean. He agitated for relief efforts to assist Ethiopia against the invasion of fascist Italy.

In the 1940s and early 1950s, James lived and worked in the United States, involving himself in socialist political organizations and learning about the black movement in this country. He recruited a young African university student named Kwame Nkrumah to join the Pan-Africanist struggle, and via his association with Padmore, helped to initiate the independence movement in the Gold Coast, now Ghana. In the late 1950s, James returned briefly to his native West Indies, leading the unsuccessful struggle to achieve political federation among the former British colonies. While in Trinidad, James brilliantly edited the independence movement's journal, and was chief adviser to leader Eric Williams, his former student.

James was a master of literature, history, political analysis, and social criticism. During his seven years in England in the thirties, he produced some of the most profound works on black liberation yet available: *A History of Negro Revolt, World Revolution,* and *The Black*

Jacobins. The *Black Jacobins* is arguably the best single historical study by a scholar of African descent in this century. The book charts the only successful slave revolution in world history, the saga of slave rebel Toussaint L'Ouverture, and the revolt in Haiti.

In a sense, history was cruel to James, as it frequently is to all political prophets. James's *Black Jacobins* was ignored at the time of its initial printing, and for two decades it was out of print entirely. James's astute political analysis went largely unread and unrecognized among black political leaders during his years in the United States. Back in Trinidad, when James raised the necessity to break with an economic and political dependency upon American imperialism, Williams broke sharply with his radical mentor. James's books were banned, and for a time he was placed under house arrest.

James will be remembered by scholars for his eloquent narrative of cultural and racial life in the Caribbean in the early 1900s, entitled *Beyond a Boundary*. His book *Nkrumah and the Ghana Revolution* is a detailed account of the triumph of African nationalist Kwame Nkrumah over British colonialism. James's *Notes on Dialectics*, written at the beginning of the Cold War, is a critique of Soviet communism and the philosophy which leads to authoritarian social control.

Why is James important to us? His intellectual legacy includes several fundamental insights. Unlike most socialists five decades ago, James argued that the black American working class had its own vitality and unique political history. He believed that the black movement was potentially the most radical of all American social movements. Second, James emphasized the central role of culture, including sports as well as literature, to our understanding of political change. And most importantly, James was a radical democrat. He opposed all forms of censorship, and advocated full democratic rights for all, whether in capitalist or communist countries. I was fortunate to have met James, and to have spent a day with him two years ago, discussing politics.

James would stand side by side with the Chinese students in Beijing who struggled for democracy. He would be with us in our struggle against racism and economic inequality here in the United States. James will be remembered as a fighter for black freedom and democracy.

June 1989

The Legacy of Huey P. Newton

The recent brutal murder of Huey P. Newton in Oakland has been used as a metaphor for the nihilism and ultimate futility of black militancy. In a predictable editorial, the *New York Times* pontificated that the co-founder and leader of the Black Panther Party was a self-destructive "prisoner of the Oakland ghetto streets where he grew up." Other Black Panther leaders had successfully made the transition to the middle class and political conformity, but not the "melancholy" Newton. "He was in and out of prison, in and out of court, in and out of drugs and alcohol abuse." The message is clear: Newton, and not the system he struggled against, was responsible for his demise.

Nearly a quarter of a century has passed since two young, militant black men, influenced by the uncompromising example of Malcolm X, discussed creating a political formation for self-defense in an anti-poverty office located in East Oakland. Huey P. Newton was five years younger than his friend Bobby Seale, yet the charismatic Newton developed as the principal leader and spokesperson for the Black Panthers and their youthful cadre. Their black leather jackets, outlandish rhetoric and tendency to parade with guns gave them an image of urban guerrillas. But an analysis of their original "Ten Point Program" reveals that their immediate objectives were reformist, rather than revolutionary.

The Black Panthers called for self-determination, the right of any people or nation which has been oppressed historically or politically dominated. They insisted upon full employment, decent housing, an end to police brutality and violations of civil rights, educational reforms, and "freedom for all black men held in federal, state, county, and city prisons and jails." With the exception of the last statement, nothing demanded by the Panthers really represented a cry for the violent overthrow of the American legal system, political economy or the power elite of white males who control the wealth and property within this society. The Black Panthers did not attack policemen patrolling the black community without cause, and did nothing to provoke armed assaults against white individuals or white-owned property within the black community.

By late 1967, the Black Panthers had initiated a free breakfast program for black children, and were offering medical services to ghetto residents without charge. And, unlike many Black Power-inspired groups, which took the simplistic view that all whites, regardless of their social class or political ideology, were the enemy, the Panthers took direct steps to link their struggle for black self-determination to the broader currents of social change within American society and throughout the world. They coalesced with white student and community activists who opposed America's illegal and immoral war in Vietnam, and called for the development of a progressive united front between all oppressed peoples of color and reform-minded whites to transform this country's economic and political system.

The Panthers consisted of several thousand idealistic and dedicated young men and women. Some within this activist formation had political experience in previous organizations—for instance, the leader of the Student Nonviolent Coordinating Committee, Stokely Carmichael, became the Panthers' Prime Minister in 1968; SNCC organizer James Forman and activist H. Rap Brown also worked briefly with the Panthers. But most of these young black militants, still in their teens and twenties, had little grounding in political strategy and tactics, organizational and technical expertise. Errors were inevitable. Women were, too frequently, relegated to secondary-level tasks, and sexism within the ranks was a serious problem. The internal structure of the party didn't adequately permit full democratic discussion and participation of the members, which created a near cult-like allegiance surrounding Huey. The Party never encouraged fully a good comprehension of political education, so members could be confused and alienated with shifts in the formation's political line. The tight, autocratic structure actually assisted the police and governmental agencies to infiltrate and manipulate Panther locals.

No error ever committed by Newton and the Black Panthers, however, can begin to equal the massive crimes carried out by the U.S. government in the name of law and order. By July 1969, the Black Panthers had been targeted by 233 separate actions under the FBI's Counter-Intelligence Program. In 1969 alone, 27 Panthers were killed by the police, and 749 were jailed or arrested. The FBI deliberately manipulated black nationalist groups to assault the Panthers, sometimes with murderous consequences. In Chicago, Panther leaders Fred Hampton and Mark Clark were murdered by police in a planned raid. And in early 1970, the FBI ordered its field offices to "counteract any favorable support in publicity to the Panthers" by placing anti-Panther propaganda in the media. During these years, Newton was shot, imprisoned, and in exile. That he survived at all, despite this massive conspiracy, is remarkable.

Huey Newton was no saint. A decade before his death, he had acquired a reputation in Oakland as violent and unpredictable. Like all political visionaries, he was a part of his political environment, and was hardened by the murderous assaults committed against his friends and associates by his government. But Newton offered a path of liberation to his generation of young African Americans, especially young black men. Instead of falling victim to gangs and black-against-black violence, Newton encouraged young people to organize for justice and community control. While black elected officials told African-American youth that the system was inherently just, if only given a chance to work, Newton correctly called for the transformation of power relationships within society. Poverty, ignorance, homelessness and hunger could not be destroyed, Newton argued, unless the oppressed seized the reins of power. Despite his personal shortcomings and weaknesses, Newton's central insight still remains correct. Huey P. Newton should be remembered as a contributor to the struggle for black freedom.

September 1989

The Legacy
of Martin Luther King

Martin Luther King, Jr., has been dead for nearly a generation. The political environment which defined his activities, the oppressive conditions of legal segregation and political disfranchisement, no longer exist. It is easy, therefore, for those who had opposed the democratic social vision of Dr. King while he was alive, such as President Bush, to provide platitudes about racial equality and justice. In the wreckage of the destruction of the U.S. Civil Rights Commission, the absence of enforcement for affirmative action and equal opportunity legislation, and the policy of ignoring the mounting tragedies of black unemployment, homelessness and growing poverty, most white American politicians hide behind the soothing image of King as an advocate of racial peace. They fear the disturbing implications of King's economic and social demands for restructuring America's social order in the final years of his life, and pretend that this final, radical phase of his political career never existed.

Black politicians have a different responsibility to be truthful within African-American history. To be sure, Martin symbolized the struggle to desegregate the racist South to dismantle the structures of civil inequality. His famous "I Have a Dream" speech, given on the steps of the Lincoln Memorial on that hot August afternoon in 1963, spoke for the democratic sacrifices and struggles of millions of African Americans, from the abolitionists like Frederick Douglass and Sojourner Truth to the early civil rights crusaders like Dr. W.E.B. Du Bois, A. Philip Randolph, and Ida B. Wells. Black elected officials and all blacks who had gained some degree of success within the cultural, social and political hierarchy of white America owe part of their accomplishment to King and thousands of other nameless freedom fighters, who demanded a redefinition of democracy beyond the color line.

But civil rights was not the only issue to divide America in the 1960s. Under the Johnson administration, the United States had sent over one-half million troops to Southeast Asia. Black Americans represented one out of seven soldiers in Vietnam, and suffered disproportionately high casualties because they were unfairly ordered into combat units. While the NAACP and Urban League, fearing political retaliation, cautioned against civil rights involvement in the Vietnam War debate, King made the decision to align his political beliefs with his ethical hatred of war. Against bitter attacks, Martin urged black Americans to reject American imperialism abroad, and the sterile logic of crusading anti-communism. King inspired millions to oppose the United States war effort.

But Martin's political legacy transcended the issue of Vietnam. He began to recognize that the political program of integration was insufficient to achieve the material basis of equality for people of color within the United States. He began to call for the nationalization of basic industries, in order to guarantee jobs for the central cities. Martin favored a plan for a guaranteed income for all Americans, and expanded social programs. To finance this domestic reconstruction, massive reductions in the Pentagon budget would be required. American foreign policy abroad would have to pull back from its support for imperialism, economic exploitation and political domination.

Martin's political vision also makes sense for the 1990s. We must advocate certain socioeconomic prerequisites for full participation in a democracy, such as the human right to a job, the human right not to starve, the right to decent housing and free medical care. Martin would insist that the battle against racism today is being lost, and that all Americans lose when blacks' median incomes are barely 55 percent those of whites. Poverty is directly connected with urban crime. And the answer to urban chaos, Martin would tell us, is not more police and capital punishment. The termination of drugs, crime and social unrest will come about only with the total reconstruction of the central cities, requiring the cancellation of billions of dollars from the military budget. The real legacy of Martin Luther King, Jr. demands a rededication to the struggle to create both a political and economic democracy in America.

January 1990

The Tragedy of Marion Barry

For months, the media followed the controversial trial of Washington, D.C. Mayor Marion Barry with a perverse mixture of fascination and disgust. Sex, drugs and public illegality always sells; the Barry trial had it all. Acting as a legal pimp, the federal government obtained the services of Barry's ex-girlfriend, Rasheeda Moore, to snag its victim. Ample evidence was presented in the trial proving to most observers that Barry had been a casual user of drugs for many years. Evidence of government malfeasance was abundant as well. Scores of Barry lieutenants and confidants had been indicted and convicted of various crimes during the past decade.

The political circus came to a disappointing end, however, when the jury found the mayor guilty of only one misdemeanor—possessing cocaine. It acquitted him of one count, and couldn't agree on twelve additional charges. Barry now claims that he was vindicated, and has announced plans to run as an independent for a D.C. Council seat.

Marion Barry is surely guilty of many things—dependence on cocaine, infidelity to his long-suffering and silent wife, and most of all, political stupidity. But the Barry case makes no sense outside of its broader political and racial context. The federal government's entire case rested on entrapment of the worst kind. No one seriously believes that Barry's decision to enter a hotel room with his former lover was dictated by a desire for crack. Sex, not drugs, motivated the mayor. Barry's certainly guilty of adultery, and his libido is out of control. His problems with alcohol and cocaine certainly made him unfit to hold public office. But the authorities would have been wiser to pressure Barry to resign, in lieu of facing criminal charges and a protracted and disruptive court trial. Instead, they were determined to place the black Democrat in a federal prison.

Barry's central argument which attempted to justify his behavior was the thesis that a pattern of FBI and judicial harassment exists against African-American civil rights leaders and elected officials. The argument is certainly true, based on the evidence over nearly half a century. In my own research on a political biography of black American leader Malcolm X, I have uncovered an extensive pattern of illegal electronic surveillance, the opening of private mail without warrants, and political harassment. COINTELPRO, the FBI's Counterintelligence Program in the sixties, plotted the destruction of civil rights organizations, and led to the imprisonment of hundreds of black activists. In the 1980s, hundreds of black elected officials, judges and other community leaders were subjected disproportionately to surveillance and harassment. Congressperson John Conyers and other members of the Congressional Black Caucus have investigated many instances of political harassment aimed at blacks. The goal is to reduce African-American political clout within the system, and to intimidate leaders to back away from challenging the establishment.

But the real tragedy of Marion Barry lies not in his cocaine dependency, which he shares with literally millions of white, hispanic and black Americans. His tragedy is his inability to place his community's objective interests ahead of his own. By his series of errors and criminal acts, Barry has set back the drive for D.C. statehood by years. His behavior provides justification for racists and political reactionaries to undermine other African-American leaders. But Barry's greatest tragedy was his failure of vision. The great strength of the black freedom struggle's political tradition, from Frederick Douglass to Martin Luther King, Jr., was the linkage between politics and ethics. What was morally correct was also politically correct. Barry's contempt for the ethics of the black struggle, his contempt for his wife, children and constituents, could never be justified. The only real service that Marion Barry could perform would be to withdraw permanently from public life.

September 1990

Black Conservatives, Shelby Steele, and the War against Affirmative Action

Throughout the twentieth century, the system has frequently relied on black conservative politicians and intellectuals to justify patterns of race and class inequality. A century ago, black educator Booker T. Washington called for "separate but equal" race relations throughout the South, justifying political disfranchisement and segregated public accommodations. Washington was intensely popular among northern capitalists and Republicans because he urged blacks to work as "scabs" undermining labor unions, and he urged African Americans not to agitate publicly for civil rights.

During the civil rights movement, there were conservative blacks who attempted to undermine Martin Luther King, Jr., and the struggle against racism. Some were privately financed by white conservatives; others genuinely believed that social change should occur gradually, rather than from civil disobedience or economic boycotts.

Corporate America has always recognized the ideological and social class diversity within the African-American community, especially the tendency of the black petty bourgeoisie to support policies which promoted capital formation and ownership. At the 1968 Black Power Conference held in Philadelphia, for example, the head of the Clairol corporation endorsed the gathering, declaring that the demand for Black Power really meant "equity, empowerment—the ownership of apartments, ownership of homes (and) ownership of businesses" for the African-American elite. A decade later, when Gulf Oil Corporation was being boycotted by African-American activists for its

212

financial support of the repressive Portuguese colonial government, the multinational responded by attempting to coopt influential blacks. It funnelled $50,000 to Reverend Ralph David Abernathy, assistant to King and head of the Southern Christian Leadership Conference; $55,000 to Reverend Leon Sullivan's Opportunities Industrialization Centers; and hundreds of thousands of additional dollars to other black cultural groups and civic leaders. In 1980, the Republicans cultivated several groups of conservative middle-class blacks, in an effort to expand its political base inside the African-American community. A group of civil rights leaders, including Abernathy and Georgia state legislator Hosea Williams, publicly endorsed Reagan. NAACP head, Benjamin Hooks, a closet Republican and former Nixon administration appointee, was invited to speak to the Republican convention on prime time, and he used this opportunity to give a panegyric on the virtues of black capitalism.

More influential was the identification of a small current of black academics with personal ambitions, who were amenable to the Republican Party's policies. The first important gathering of this group occurred in late 1980, under the auspices of the Institute of Contemporary Studies, a reactionary think tank. The key sponsors were two conservative black economists, Thomas Sowell of the Hoover Institution, and Walter Williams, currently a professor at George Mason University. Guests and participants included journalist/entrepreneur Tony Brown, Republican newspaper columnist and former Black Power advocate Chuck Stone, *Black Power* coauthor Charles V. Hamilton, and former Manhattan borough president and businessperson Percy Sutton. Sowell established the general line of this gathering by advocating positions against affirmative action, liberal social welfare programs, and the minimum wage.

Throughout the 1980s, the black neo-conservative current expanded significantly, nurtured by the Reagan administration's desire to counter charges that its policies were racist. Some of the principal ideologues were: Sowell; Williams; Glenn C. Loury, professor at Harvard's Kennedy School of Government; J.A.Y. Parker, president of the Lincoln Institute for Research and Education; Robert Woodson, president of the National Association of Neighborhood Enterprises; and Joseph Perkins, editorial writer for the *Wall Street Journal*. In government, the top black Reaganites were Clarence Pendleton, controversial head of the U.S. Civil Rights Commission, and Clarence Thomas, the chairman of the Equal Employment Opportunity Commission. In the early 1980s, Sowell was clearly the most widely-quoted and influential spokesperson for this group; by the mid-1980s Loury had surpassed him, and was being groomed as Assistant Secretary of Education under conservative politician William Bennett. Loury's personal peccadilloes with the law in Massachusetts prohibited him from gaining this policy position. Both Sowell and Loury suffered from personal reputations for arrogance, and abrasive political styles designed to win few converts. Moreover, both were somewhat flawed by their earlier political and ideological commitments: Loury had been a liberal Democrat only a decade before, and Sowell claimed to be a Marxist well into his thirties.

With the election of Bush, a tactical shift occurred. A "kinder and gentler" approach toward the "Negro Question" was initiated. Unlike Reagan, who never failed to display his utter contempt of the African-American community, Bush was properly coached in the liberal discourse of the civil rights movement. In Reagan's eight years in office, he met briefly with representatives of the black community a total of eight times; by comparison, Bush has caucused with leaders from the Congressional Black Caucus, civil rights formations and black neo-conservatives at least 40 times since early 1989. Bush praised Nelson Mandela's courageous struggle against apartheid, and he embraced the legacy of Martin Luther King, Jr.

rhetorically. These efforts were not lost upon the majority of African-Americans, as Bush's approval ratings in public opinion polls reached record levels for any Republican president. Considering the undisguised racism of his predecessor in the Oval Office, Bush's rather modest response to blacks' interests appeared unduly magnified, almost liberal and enlightened.

But style does not reflect substance. Bush continues the repressive policies of Reagan towards black-oriented policy questions. His administration's foreign policies treat non-western societies with scarcely veiled disregard. For example, Poland and Hungary were slated for $900 million in U.S. foreign aid; newly-independent Namibia was allocated one-half million dollars, and Jamaica's aid was actually cut $18 million to provide greater assistance to subsidize the restoration of capitalism in Eastern Europe. On the domestic front, Bush proposes little to nothing to address widespread African-American unemployment, cutbacks in public transportation and inadequately funded public housing and education programs.

Civil rights enforcement also continues to be curtailed. The Education Department's Office for Civil Rights, for example, recently stopped its staff members travelling to conduct compliance investigations or to review universities which had already been found violating civil rights laws. Bush nominated Clarence Thomas for a seat on the United States Court of Appeals for the District of Columbia, a step widely viewed as positioning the black conservative as the replacement for elderly liberal Associate Justice Thurgood Marshall on the Supreme Court. But the most important element of Bush's offensive against civil rights is the administration's continued hostility and opposition towards affirmative action programs, which seek to redress historic patterns of discrimination in employment and education for women and people of color. Bush's position was strengthened by the recent

Wards Cove Packing v. Antonio decision, which declared that the under-representation of blacks and other minorities in the workplace is not *prima facie* evidence of racism. To prove discrimination, one must now show that the criteria employed in the selection of workers was clearly biased, with the intent of excluding minorities.

The most recent neo-conservative star to appear on the political horizon is Shelby Steele, an English professor at San Jose State University. In a series of public statements, television appearances, and in excerpts from his soon-to-be published book, *The Content of Our Character*, Steele advances a more sophisticated version of the Sowell-Loury thesis attacking affirmative action and the current legislative and legal agenda of civil rights advocates. Steele's newfound prominence as a media and policy critic must first be analyzed on its own terms, with a critique of its central premises. Secondly, Steele's work must be understood within the current political and economic conjuncture.

Steele's first criticism about the use of affirmative action programs is historical. He observed recently in the *New York Times* that "the 1964 civil-rights bill was passed on the understanding that equal opportunity would not mean racial preference. But in the late 60s and early 70s, affirmative action underwent a remarkable escalation of its mission from simple anti-discrimination enforcement to social engineering by means of quotas, goals, timetables, set-asides and other forms of preferential treatment."

Steele's basic insight is partially correct. The majority of civil rights leaders were racial integrationists, women and men who believed in the goal of a "color blind" society, a social order in which racial identity would become irrelevant. The *Brown v. Board of Education* decision of 1954, which legally outlawed the segregation of public schools, argued that any form of racial separatism was *de facto* evidence of discrimination. The ruling declared, "To separate Negro children solely because of their race generates a feeling of inferiority as to their status in the community that might affect their hearts and minds in a way unlikely ever to be undone." This color-blind ideology was adopted and reinterpreted by the legal profession as a theory of race neutrality, which disconnected race from social relations or economic condition. Associate Justice Anton Scalia's dissent in the *Richmond v. Croson* case provides an example. Scalia comments: "the relevant proposition is not that it was blacks, or Jews or Irish who were discriminated against, but that it was individual men and women, 'created equal,' who were discriminated against." In other words, the reality of race is accidental, rather than socially constructed or politically determined.

King echoed this interpretation of race in his most famous address, delivered at the August 1963 March on Washington: "I have a dream that my four little children will one day live in a nation where they will not be judged by the color of their skin but by the content of their character." With this quotation, unlike Sowell and his conservative epigones, Steele attempts to place himself as an ideological comrade of King and opponent of so-called racism within the white and black communities alike. What this ignores completely is that there was always another tendency within the struggle for black equality, represented by W.E.B. Du Bois and others, who insisted that the goal was not color blindness, but cultural pluralism within a democratic and humane social order. To uproot racism, Du Bois argued, race-conscious remedies were necessary. This perspective gradually won out, even among the reformist integrationists within the NAACP and Urban League, who recognized, by the time of the Nixon administration, that it was not enough to dismantle the structures of formal segregation. Measures had to be taken to ensure that blacks, Latinos, women and others who had experienced systemic discrimination received compensatory justice.

Steele insists that the imposition of affirmative action goals and timetables creates a false sense of pluralism and equality inside campuses. "Racial preferences allow society to leapfrog over the difficult problem of developing blacks to parity with whites and into a cosmetic diversity that covers the blemish of disparity," Steele asserts. In short, most African Americans are not culturally or intellectually prepared to compete with whites on an equal basis. Their premature advancement into highly competitive educational or vocational positions represented a type of "cosmetic diversity," which failed to unearth the root causes for black "deprivation."

Here, Steele unthinkingly draws from an older ideological tradition of black conservatism, the rhetoric of Booker T. Washington. It was the architect of black capitalism and accommodation to lynching who proclaimed, a century ago: "Ignorance and inexperience, it is not strange that in the first years of our new life" after slavery that blacks "began at the top instead of at the bottom; that a seat in Congress or the state legislature was more sought than real estate or industrial skill." Both Steele and Washington imply that blacks are not intellectually or socially ready to assume their rightful share of power. In the meantime, they carve out for themselves the role of brokers between the "undeveloped" black masses and the white capitalist power structure.

Finally, Steele resorts to a social psychological argument against affirmative action. Racial quotas which discriminate against "innocent whites" create two destructive social dynamics, Steele argues. Whites draw the conclusion that all blacks, regardless of their abilities, achieve position or status solely due to their racial category. Blacks "feel a stab of horror," Steele pontificates, because they detest being viewed in this manner. "The effect of preferential treatment—the lowering of normal standards to increase black representation—puts blacks at war with an expanded realm of debilitating doubt, so that the doubt itself becomes an unrecognized preoccupation that undermines their ability to perform, especially in integrated situations."

Steele's social psychological critique has been eagerly seized upon both by white conservatives, who had always opposed affirmative action anyway, and by weary white liberals who have retreated from the problems of the ghetto. Journalist Charles Krauthammer, writing in the *Washington Post,* for example, praised "Steele's view on this terrible psychic toll of affirmative action." In short, "affirmative action costs more than it is worth—It dispenses unequal justice. It balkanizes communities. It distorts the merit system—and now, it attaches a question mark to every real black achievement."

There are several ways to illustrate the intellectual bankruptcy of Steele's arguments. For example, one could focus solely on the slippery concept of "merit" as the criterion for employment selection or admission to college or medical school. The criteria for determining merit in any situation are based largely on the leadership of a given institution and its dominant ideology. If women and people of color are systematically denied positions of authority within a particular field, or if their intellectual contributions to the subject are ignored, the field becomes "biased" in its core methodology and criteria for what comprises excellence. Thus, to circumvent the problem, the criteria for merit must be restructured to include the values of gender and racial diversity.

Another argument against Steele's meritocracy is that provided by black radical theologian Cornel West, in his 1986 essay, "Assessing Black Neoconservatism." The false debate of "merit v. race" obscures the fact that "job hiring choices are both meritorious *and* personal choices," West observes. "And this personal dimension often is influenced by racist perceptions. Within the practical world of U.S. employment practices, the new black conservative rhetoric about race-free meritorious criteria does no more than justify actual practices of racial discrimination against blacks."

Perhaps the most telling criticism of Steele's thesis is that he fails to correctly define or describe institutional racism. For Steele, racial discrimination is an irrational relic of the past, essentially a form of archaic behavior linked to segregation. This ignores the rising tide of racist incidents and harassment experienced by black college students, or the racism manifested in the streets against African Americans and other people of color. Racism is not irrational. Racism is part of a political and economic system of domination, structurally linked to capitalism, and perpetuated in the power and privileges which a small minority of Americans exercise over the vast majority of people. Racism is an index on the continuing patterns of economic, educational and political inequality which are experienced by African Americans, despite the removal of Jim Crow segregation signs.

Steele symbolizes a real turning point in the façade of institutional racism in American life. The old system of Jim Crow no longer serves the goals of capitalism. Demographically, American society is becoming increasingly multi-ethnic; within 30 years, about half of the adult labor force between the ages of 25 and 54 will be nonwhite. A new system of domination is emerging which employs the post-civil rights discourse of equal opportunity within the framework of a capitalist political economy. Increasingly, elements of the Latino, Asian and black petty bourgeoisie are being absorbed and assimilated into the secondary ranks of the corporate, educational and political establishments.

The ideology of affirmative action is potentially threatening because it speaks to the specific grievances and historical claims for material equality and social justice of various exploited groups. As these constituencies gain in numbers and potential power, their capacity to challenge the hegemonic ideology of individualism, materialism and Eurocentrism also increases. To fragment the ranks of the opposition, ideologues like Steele are brought to the forefront, preaching a mythical meritocracy which has never actually existed even for white, property-owning males.

So long as racial discrimination and class exploitation exist, we should anticipate a series of Shelby Steeles, one after another, in defense of the status quo. Our task is to recognize always that just behind such ideologues, partially hidden by their rhetoric, exists a powerful political and economic apparatus, motivated by profit and perpetuated by racism, hatred and fear. We should not be so preoccupied with the ruminations of the Shelby Steeles that we lose sight of those larger forces which have created them.

June 1990

Clarence Thomas:
Black Conservative
for the Supreme Court?

George Bush's selection of Judge Clarence Thomas to replace Associate Justice Thurgood Marshall on the Supreme Court represents a clever assault against the entire civil rights movement. By choosing Thomas, an African American, Bush believes that he makes it difficult for progressives to oppose his candidate's record.

Superficially, Thomas's life seems to be a rags to riches story. Born in Savannah, Georgia, in deep poverty, Thomas was educated by the charity of white Catholic nuns. He sacrificed and struggled to obtain a Yale law degree. But his rise from poverty to power really occurred as the aide of Republican Senator John Danforth of Missouri. It was under Danforth's influence that the ambitious Black attorney's political views swung sharply to the right.

With Danforth's backing, Thomas was appointed head of the Equal Employment Opportunity Commission during the Reagan administration. During his seven year tenure, Thomas alienated African Americans and other liberal constituencies by opposing affirmative action goals and timetables. Thomas rejected the basic economic agenda of the civil rights movement, by attacking federal initiatives for full employment and expanded social programs. But his most outrageous act occurred in 1988, when he criticized the famous 1954 *Brown v. Board of Education* decision, which outlawed racially segregated public schools. In supreme arrogance, Thomas declared that the decision was based on "dubious social science." If Thomas had been in Montgomery, Alabama back in 1955, he probably would have sat quietly in the segregated section of that city's buses, instead of protesting along with Rosa Parks and Martin Luther King, Jr.

Thomas is also deeply opposed to women's rights issues, particularly the freedom of choice on abortion. Several years ago, Thomas commented favorably on an article which strongly condemned abortion rights. And in two separate articles, Thomas attacked the 1965 Supreme Court ruling *Griswold v. Connecticut,* which later became part of the legal justification for women's freedom of choice on abortion.

Despite Thomas's conservative political credentials, it will be difficult to mount a successful campaign to block his appointment to the Supreme Court. Thomas is actually the black ideological twin of David Souter, Bush's first nominee to the high court. Mediocrity, not legal vision or moral compassion, is the outstanding characteristic of both men.

Like Souter, Thomas is no intellectual. Most of his meager published articles are polemics against "racial quotas" and affirmative action. He has written almost nothing on other important constitutional issues. Thomas's silence on these issues permits him to follow Souter's footsteps as the so-called "stealth nominee" to the Supreme Court.

The basic legal strategy employed by Bush is simply an extension of the reactionary agenda of Ronald Reagan. During Bush's first two years as president, he appointed 70 federal judges, nearly all of whom were white, affluent males. Less than 12 percent of Bush's federal judges have been females; only 6.5 percent have been minorities. Nearly all of his selections have been hostile to environmental protection laws, civil liberties, the rights of criminal defendants, and abortion rights. This represents an aggressive, conservative agenda to use the court system to destroy progressive democratic movements for reform, and to return African Americans, hispanics, women and others to second-class status.

Bush was so determined to pursue these conservative goals that he deliberately avoided considering "moderate" Republican judges. One example would be Judge Amalye Kearse, and African-American Republican currently serving on the federal appeals court in New York. Kearse's moderate political views, however, made her unacceptable to dogmatic ideologues within the Bush administration.

Even the *Wall Street Journal,* no friend of civil rights and women's equality, has candidly interpreted the meaning of Thurgood Marshall's resignation from the Supreme Court. The *Journal* predicted that Bush would "nominate a conservative committed to continuing the court's restriction of abortion rights, its crackdown on the rights of the accused and its narrowing of other civil liberties." With the selection of Clarence Thomas, Bush continues to advance a form of radical conservatism, repudiating the legal legacy of Thurgood Marshall. If confirmed by the Senate, Thomas would become part of a monolithic conservatism in the nation's highest court, threatening the entire struggle for equal justice in our country.

July 1991

Thurgood Marshall and the Continuing Struggle for Equality

During his quarter century on the Supreme Court, Justice Thurgood Marshall represented the voice of the most oppressed sectors of American society—African Americans, Latinos, the poor, and prisoners. Marshall's departure from the court represents the end of an entire era of American political history, a period of democratic protest in which reformers used the legal system to challenge racial, gender and social inequality. To appreciate fully the legal sea change which occurred, one should consider the fact that the two remaining "liberals" on the Supreme Court, Republican Justices Harry A. Blackmun and John Paul Stevens, were appointed respectively by Presidents Nixon and Ford. Marshall's resignation, states Harvard Law professor Laurence H. Tribe, means "there is no one there who has the slightest idea of what it's like to be seriously oppressed, segregated, the victim of relentless prejudice and who has not led a life of privilege."

The roots of Marshall's vision of legal equality are found within his personal and political history. Born on July 2, 1908, the younger of two sons of a Pullman railroad car porter and school teacher, young Marshall graduated from Douglass High School in Baltimore, and enrolled at Lincoln University in Pennsylvania. Both parents reinforced within him the expectation of achievement and self-confidence. His mother pawned her wedding ring and other items to help pay for her son's tuition. Marshall attended classes and studied by day, and worked half-time at odd jobs, including work as a busboy, grocery clerk, and waiter. In 1929, Thurgood graduated with honors.

Thurgood's father, William Marshall, was responsible for convincing his son to pursue a legal career. He repeatedly told his son to oppose racism wherever he encountered it, despite the repercussions. In later life, Marshall quoted his father as stating: "Son, if anyone ever calls you a nigger, you not only got my permission to fight him you got my orders to fight him." He attempted to enroll into the University of Maryland Law School but was immediately rejected solely on racial grounds. Marshall decided to attend Howard University Law School, where he quickly rose to the top of his class as an articulate and aggressive student. In one instance, during evening sessions at Howard Law School Library when NAACP leaders Walter White and Charles Hamilton Houston were planning legal strategy in a desegregation case, White was "amazed" at the curt behavior of one "lanky, brash law student who was always present." White later wrote: "But I soon learned of his great value to the case and doing everything he was asked [including] research on obscure legal options... This law student was Thurgood Marshall." In 1933, Marshall was awarded the LL.B degree *magna cum laude.* One of his first actions as the legal counsel of the NAACP chapter in Baltimore was to force the University of Maryland Law School to admit its first African-American student in 1935.

During the Great Depression, Marshall developed his private practice in Baltimore by taking on difficult civil rights cases. One friend at the time noted that Marshall had "built the largest law practice in Baltimore and still couldn't pay his rent." The crusading young attorney became Houston's chief lieutenant in the legal department of the NAACP, and was appointed Houston's successor in 1938. During the next 16 years, Marshall was the field commander in the legal assault against Jim Crow segregation. In a series of brilliant legal maneuvers, Marshall successfully argued case after case before the Supreme Court, winning 29 out of 32 cases. In 1947, in the suit of Herman Sweatt, Marshall forced the University of Texas to admit an African-American man to its law school. But the most important victory occurred on the issue of racial segregation in the public schools. Challenging the influential constitutional attorney, John W. Davis, Marshall argued before the Supreme Court that racial segregation was a direct violation of an African American's constitutional rights. By segregating the public schools, Marshall argued, "Slavery is perpetuated." The high court agreed. On May 17, 1954, the U.S. Supreme Court unanimously ruled that racial segregation in public schools was unconstitutional. The ruling declared: "To separate Negro children solely because of their race generates a feel of inferiority as to their status in the community that may affect their hearts and minds in a way unlikely ever to be undone... We conclude that in the field of public education the doctrine of 'separate but equal' has no place." The *Brown v. Board of Education* decision proved the legal rationale for the upsurgence of civil rights activism of the 1950s and 1960s, symbolized by the work of Martin Luther King, Jr.

Marshall's desegregation activities in the courtroom often placed himself in jeopardy. In 1946, after successfully defending several African Americans accused of attempted murder in a rural Tennessee town, he was stopped by police and searched for liquor. Finding none, the police, with guns drawn, arrested Marshall for drunken driving. After returning to town, the police ordered Marshall to walk across the street to the magistrate's office. Marshall sensed a setup. Throughout the South during Jim Crow, hundreds of African-American men and women had been shot in the back by police supposedly for attempting to escape arrest. Marshall refused to go unless he had a police escort. Since Marshall obviously wasn't drunk, the magistrate promptly freed him.

Throughout the 1950s Marshall shared the political

perspective of NAACP leaders Walter White and Roy
Wilkins. He was a staunch integrationist, who believed
that equality could not be achieved for African-Americans
unless all forms of cultural, social and economic separation between whites and African Americans were eliminated. He favored legal challenges to segregation rather
than street demonstrations, boycotts and direct action, a
gradual rather than a military strategy. "It's only by law
suits and legislation," Marshall declared in 1947, "that
we'll ever teach reactionaries the meaning of the Fourteenth Amendment." Before King initiated the massive
nonviolent campaigns, Marshall warned against the use
of "disobedience" against segregation, declaring that this
would culminate "in wholesale slaughter with no good
achieved." Similarly, Marshall was unsympathetic with
those voices in the African-American community who
called for nationalist solutions. He directly condemned the
militancy of Malcolm X and attacked the Nation of Islam
in a 1959 speech at Princeton University. The Black
Muslims were "run by a bunch of thugs organized from
prisons and jails, and financed, I am sure by [Egyptian
President] Gamal Abdel Nasser or some Arab group."
Malcolm correctly responded that the struggle for African-
American liberation was not confined solely to the elimination of Jim Crow. "It is not a case of wanting integration
or separation," Malcolm stated, "it is a case of wanting
freedom, justice, and equality. It is not integration that
Negroes in America want, it is human dignity." Although
Marshall has devoted his entire life to struggle, he was
still unable to recognize the full dimensions and complex-
ity of institutional racism and class domination inside the
United States. His legal victories had given him too much
confidence in the ultimate justice and fairness of the legal
and political system.

In 1961, President Kennedy appointed Marshall as
judge of the U.S. Court of Appeals for the Second Circuit.
However, segregationist Senators who hated Marshall's

legal triumphs successfully blocked his appointment for a year. During his tenure as a federal judge he wrote over 150 decisions, most of which extended civil rights and liberties. In 1965, President Johnson selected Marshall to become solicitor general, the third-highest position in the Justice Department. It was clear to all political observers that the posts were merely stepping stones for Marshall, who was finally nominated by Johnson to become a Justice on the Supreme Court in June 1967. By replacing Southern moderate Tom Clark, Marshall immediately gave liberals a solid majority on the high court behind Chief Justice Earl Warren. Despite his outstanding career, conservatives hostile to civil rights predicted that Marshall was at best a mediocre appointment to the court. The *National Review* called Marshall "competent" but "dull" and "pedestrian." Columnist Joseph Kraft warned that Marshall "will not bring to the court penetrating analysis or distinction of mind." Regardless of the legal victories and adoption of civil rights laws, even the accomplishments of a person as gifted as Marshall could not fully escape the smears and stench of white racism.

During Marshall's first years on the Court, he was perceived not as a leader, but as a steady and predictable liberal vote. He eschewed the technicalities of law for the fundamental issues, and urged his colleagues to vote according to "what is right." One liberal colleague, Justice William O. Douglas, subsequently observed that Marshall was "not one to speak up articulately or forcefully." Nevertheless, he remained quite impressive, especially on cases affecting civil rights, civil liberties, and the poor. Former Attorney General Ramsey Clark noted that "adversity challenged Thurgood Marshall." He has an "enormous passion" for civil rights and a commitment to "equal justice under the law."

Some of Marshall's greatest contributions were in the field of higher education. Marshall believed that universities had the obligation of expanding opportunities for learning to the most oppressed sectors of society. In the pivotal *Bakke v. Regents of the University of California* in 1978, in which the Supreme Court declared that colleges could employ race as a factor in admissions decisions but could not impose specific racial quotas, Marshall issued a memorable dissent. "While I applaud the judgement of the Court that a university may consider race in its admissions process," Marshall stated, "it is more than a little ironic that, after several hundred years of class-based discrimination against Negroes, the court is unwilling to hold that a class-based remedy for that discrimination is permissible." Marshall recognized that despite the passage of civil rights legislation in the 1960s, institutional racism was still pervasive throughout the social fabric of society. "It is unnecessary in twentieth century America to have individual Negroes demonstrate that they have been victims of discrimination; the racism of our society has been so pervasive that none, regardless of wealth or position, has managed to escape the impact." Marshall also was convinced that bias within the university setting was not based solely on race or gender. In 1985, he authored a decision in which the Supreme Court expanded the enforcement of anti-discriminatory laws against people with physical disabilities.

Marshall was also the strongest opponent of the death penalty on the Supreme Court throughout his tenure. In 1972, when the court outlawed the death penalty in most states, it was Marshall who served as the conscience of America. Marshall wrote: "Death is irrevocable, life imprisonment is not. Death, of course, makes rehabilitation impossible. Life imprisonment does not. In short, death had always been viewed as the ultimate sanction...In striking down capital punishment, this court does not malign our system of government. On the contrary, it pays homage to it...In recognizing the humanity of our fellow beings, we pay ourselves the highest tribute.

With the election of Ronald Reagan in 1980, the

status of the Supreme Court fundamentally changed. Conservatives who had never supported the legal reforms sparked by the civil rights movement, including equal opportunity legislation, affirmative action, under-represented racial group set-asides for economic development, and other innovations, were now in power. They sought to roll back the Second Reconstruction by placing relatively young, upper-class white males in critical positions on the U.S. Circuit Court and district court. Reagan himself made archconservative William Rehnquist Chief Justice, and was able to appoint a solid majority of conservatives on the Supreme Court. Marshall, and three embattled liberals remained on the courts, struggled to keep alive the concepts of civil rights, equal justice, and fairness. As Marshall passed his 80th birthday, Reagan conservatives, "looked longingly at Marshall's seat," waiting for his death in order to reinforce their reactionary majority. During these recent years, under the pressure of adversity, Thurgood Marshall has perhaps achieved his greatest stature. No longer the self-confident, crusading trial lawyer, Marshall finally has recognized that there is nothing inherently progressive or liberal about the Supreme Court, the Congress, or the presidency. The Supreme Court had once been the bastion of civil rights; but today, it has reverted to its pre-1940s posture of repressing the rights of the poor, working people and people of color. In a September, 1989, address before the Second Circuit Judicial Conference, Marshall noted that the Supreme Court's attitude toward civil rights was essentially hostile. In the recent *Richmond v. Croson* case, "the Court took a broad swipe at affirmative action, making it extraordinarily hard for any state or city to fashion a race-conscious remedial program that will survive its constitutional scrutiny." Marshall noted that the Supreme Court in the case of *Ward's Cove v. Atonio* now demanded that employees of color and women employees had "to prove that" employers carried out discriminatory employment practices, easing the burden on businesses. "In the past 35 years," Marshall admitted, "we have truly come full circle."

But Marshall does not advise resignation—he urges African Americans and their allies in the struggle for freedom to deepen their effort. "We must do more than dwell on past battles," Marshall declares. "History teaches that when the Supreme Court has been willing to short-change the equality rights of underrepresented ethnic groups, other basic personal civil liberties like the rights to free speech and to personal security against unreasonable searches and seizures are also threatened." In short, the battle for African-American equality and justice advances the democratic struggles and interest of all oppressed Americans. Marshall urges people to bring "pressure to bear on all branches of federal and state government" including the Supreme Court "to undertake the battles of civil liberties that remain to be won."

Thurgood Marshall's vision of democracy and equal rights has been central to the African-American struggle for freedom for a half century. Despite his earlier political contradictions and opposition to Black Power, Marshall nevertheless made essential contributions to the strategy to redefine the nature of democracy and its relationship to the most dispossessed and marginal segments of society. As Harvard Law School professor Randall Kennedy, a former law clerk of Marshall, recently declared: "[Marshall's departure] means the loss of one of the great voices in American constitutional jurisprudence, a voice that stood for values that are under tremendous threat, most important of which is equality in all of its various meanings." The legacy of Marshall provides part of the directions for a new commitment for democratic struggles for equality in the future.

July 1991

In Search of Black Leadership

Will "black leaders" exist in the twenty-first century? A generation ago, the activism of the entire African-American community revolved around one central goal—the destruction of racial segregation, and the integration of blacks into the mainstream of American political and economic institutions. For many within the black middle class, these aims were accomplished. Thousands of blacks are now corporate managers, successful entrepreneurs, politicians and professionals. Yet these examples of individual success obscure a simmering leadership crisis which could split the African-American community apart in the coming decades.

A central factor which always kept different social classes and income groups together in the black community was the commonality of our oppression. Jim Crow segregation was in essence "nondiscriminatory discrimination." Segregation affected the black middle class, blue collar workers and the unemployed equally. Blacks on welfare and Ph.D.s alike were ordered to the back of the bus, or were denied positions solely based on race. The commonality of racial oppression gave us a sense of solidarity, and intra-group dependency. Black physicians depended on patients who usually were black. African-American lawyers and accountants looked to other blacks as their potential clients.

With desegregation, the class divisions which had always existed within the black community became more intense, as many affluent African Americans no longer identified with the economic and social problems of working class and poor blacks. Many moved from the ghetto into integrated suburbs, in search of higher property values and better schools. The graduates of Howard and

Spelman began to send their daughters and sons to Harvard and Swarthmore.

In the central cities, a sense of community simultaneously has deteriorated. Millions of young women and men are trapped in a destructive system of inferior schools, violence, drugs and unemployment. The chaos is so great that more African-American young men will be murdered by other black men in the 1990s than the total number of American troops killed in Vietnam.

We cannot look to the political system, the Democrats or Republicans, or to the corporate establishment for solutions to the present crisis, because all too frequently their policies have directly contributed to our problems. Instead, we must recognize that one of the root factors in the growing class divisions and social disruption which we are experiencing is an absence of creative, dynamic leadership.

Oppressed people have never liberated themselves without leaders, women and men who have a vision and the capacity to articulate the common grievances and goals of the community. Such leaders—an Ida B. Wells, W.E.B. Du Bois, Malcolm X, Fannie Lou Hamer, Martin Luther King, Jr.—may come from many different walks of life. But what they share in common is a willingness to set aside their own personal interests to advance the objectives of the most oppressed sectors of society.

Leaders are not born, they are "made." The next phase of our struggle for freedom requires the identification of creative and energetic young women and men in our central cities. Professional blacks have the moral and political obligation to provide the resources necessary for leadership development for the next generation of black people. The leaders of the twenty-first century need a sound foundation of cultural awareness and history, as well as the technological and research skills to be productive individuals.

"Freedom Schools" could be established for young people after school and on Saturdays, with a curriculum which provides a deep social conscience, political awareness and a commitment to group advancement. There is no conflict between academic achievement in traditional terms, and the cultivation of skill in civil disobedience, voter education and mobilization.

Black professionals in corporations should promote partnership programs between their firms and urban public school systems, enriching the curricula and identifying young African Americans interested in business careers. Black religious institutions should initiate credit unions, food cooperatives and other institutions in which young people are instructed in management skills and which are designed to provide capital, food and other necessary resources to their neighbors.

Black fraternities and sororities can do more to create special training programs for young blacks interested in civil rights and social justice issues, by sponsoring internships with black public policy groups and elected officials. The focus should always be to expand the bridge between the next generation of young people from the black middle class and professionals to the problems and crises faced daily by black poor and working-class people. The linkages of service and collective obligation across income and class lines must be strengthened.

If we fail to establish this bridge, in the next century we will increasingly have "black leaders" in business, government and the legal system who are nominally black, but have absolutely no connections with the plight or problems of the majority of African Americans. Meanwhile, with the expansion of prisons, the escalation of the death penalty for nonwhites, and the increase of drugs, fragmentation and social destruction for the vast majority of blacks will continue. Without leaders with a collective vision for empowering all black people, we will continue to be oppressed.

May 1990

Chapter IX

The Challenge
of Multicultural Democracy

The Challenge of Democracy

Throughout the world today, there is a rising tide of democracy. In China during the past month, we have witnessed more than a million students and workers who demonstrated on behalf of democracy, in Tiananmen Square in Beijing. The cry for greater civil liberties and against official corruption threatened the regime of Deng Xiaoping and Prime Minister Li Peng, and a bloody repression was launched. Hundreds were killed and many wounded.

In the Soviet Union, a new legislative process has promoted mass popular approval and participation of dissidents. A new willingness to foster ideological and political pluralism is necessary in order to restructure the Soviet economy. In Hungary, there are plans to establish a genuine, multi-party state without the permanent domination of the Communist Party from the top. And in Poland, only days ago, a competitive, democratic election brought many advocates of the Solidarity labor movement into the government.

In country after country, people are demanding a greater degree of accountability by their political leaders, and more authority to determine state policies. They expect a higher degree of ethical behavior and democratic decision-making. In Washington, D.C., the crisis of ethics brought down Jim Wright, the Speaker of the House of Representatives, and Tony Coelho, Democratic House Whip. Republican Congressperson Donald Lukens was recently convicted for having sexual relations with a minor, yet he's fighting to maintain his official position. Such ethical issues raise in sharp relief the question of what citizens have a right to expect from elected officials.

The outbreak of democracy in communist nations has prompted many conservative critics to argue that the

238

competition between socialism and capitalism is finally over, and that capitalism has won. Going even further, right-wing ideologue Michael Novak insisted recently that the social-ist-inspired "dream of economic equality does not work." Since the abilities of each human being are different, Novak argued in *Forbes* magazine, each individual must receive different rewards. "Justice seems to demand diversity, not uniformity, in rewards," Novak declared. "The dream of economic equality for all is not attainable."

Progressives in America have much to learn from the Soviet experiment in *glasnost* and from the Chinese students' quest for democracy, for such examples teach us that there are many different roads to democracy. But when conservative critics tell us that such efforts disprove the necessity for equality of material conditions, we accept such a judgement at our peril. For if the civil rights movement against racial segregation taught us anything, we should have learned that the greater vision of democ-racy cannot be fulfilled simply by passing laws which permit blacks to attend whites-only schools. A viable democracy cannot exist in which two to three million people are sleeping in the gutters and streets of this nation. A viable democracy cannot exist in which 20 million Americans go to bed hungry each night, and 37 million lack any type of health or dental insurance.

Democracy is not a thing, it is a process of expanding opportunities for all citizens, and the ability to control decisionmaking from the bottom up. This requires certain prerequisites for a decent life for all within the political society—full employment, decent housing, education, health care, and so forth. The battle for full democracy leads directly and inevitably toward the promise of eco-nomic equality. The challenge for all democracies is not to make the rich richer, but for all of us to exercise greater economic and political rights.

June 1989

Why American Democracy Has Failed

Last month, the House of Representatives approved a reduction in the capital gains tax rate, giving President Bush a major legislative victory over Congressional Democrats. The bill would lower the top capital gains tax rate to 19.6 percent, from 33 percent. It would apply to all income from sales of stocks, real estate, and bonds. In effect, the wealthiest Americans—those earning over $200,000 annually—will receive 60 percent of the total tax benefits, about $25,000 per taxpayer. Americans earning above $100,000 would receive 80 percent of the benefits. This bill, an undisguised version of welfare for the rich, was praised by Bush's Treasury Secretary Nicholas F. Brady, for "strengthening America's economy, creating new jobs and giving America's small businesses and entrepreneurs a fair chance to compete internationally." Even during the high tide of Reaganism, it would be hard to imagine a more naked, aggressive and vicious assault against working class, middle-income, and poor people.

Although the status of the capital gains tax bill remains in doubt, the fact remains that one-third of the Congressional Democrats abandoned their leadership. The vote reveals that a solid Congressional majority still exists which blindly follows the economic dogma characteristic of Reaganism. The rationale that cutting taxes of the wealthy will provide jobs to the poor is only a crude scheme for expanding poverty. The philosophy behind this vote is that the government has no obligation to any significant segment of society except the economic ruling class.

When working people witness this unvarnished grab for profits, the question arises: "What are the *real* values which inform the policies of America's political system?" Let us reflect upon the actual uses and abuses of power within the current political process. But to do so, we must take the perspective not of the privileged elites whose pockets will sag from this tax cut, but from the increasingly marginalized sectors of the middle and working classes.

American democracy has failed because it is motivated by the notion of the zero-sum game, that there are winners and losers only. The rule of human fairness, a desire to create equitable conditions between groups and individuals, is transcended by individual gain at the expense of the common good.

American democracy has failed because of its institutionalized tendency to ignore the long-term sufferings of millions of American people, the homeless, the poor, people of color and working people. When the powerful and the privileged make demands, both parties listen and respond. Where is the political party which represents the material interests of the majority of us, the women and men who work every day, who make the goods and provide the services? When Latinos and African Americans call for prompt action against racism, poverty and inferior education, Bush is blind and the vast majority of Congress is deaf.

American democracy has failed because the political system and the power elite of this country would rather have the omnipresent threat of nuclear war rather than make earnest efforts to build upon the peace initiatives of the Soviet Union. Days ago, Deputy Secretary of State Lawrence Eagleburger declared: "for all its risks and uncertainties, the Cold War was characterized by a remarkably stable and predictable set of relations among the great powers." In short, why does the Bush administration despise Gorbachev, and why is it nostalgic for the Cold War? Gorbachev has the political courage to transcend the military stalemate and nuclear terror of four decades, but Bush has no comparable vision. His advisers recognize that to close the door on the Cold War would mean an inevitable reduction in the billions allocated to the Pentagon. It would deny the powerful a crucial tool which has been used to structure national policies in favor of private profits and against human needs.

Our challenge is to create a new definition of democracy, a majoritarian agenda of jobs, peace and justice. What's at stake is the future of democracy itself.

October 1989

Building Multiracial
Political Coalitions

In recent months, there have been numerous media reports about Asian-black tensions in many urban areas. The well-publicized economic boycott by black activists against Korean merchants in Brooklyn's Flatbush neighborhood is projected superficially as a manifestation of "black racism." Unfortunately, black leaders have not done enough to examine the areas of possible political and economic unity between African Americans and other people of color—including hispanics, American Indians, and Pacific Americans.

Neither the NAACP nor the Congressional Black Caucus, for example, maintain continuing dialogues with Puerto Rican and Chicano organizations. In many cities, black-hispanic political relations have become more fractious than fraternal, as the latter have grown dramatically in number and political clout over the past decade. Cooperation between hispanic and black caucuses in most state legislatures and city councils is at best inconsistent. African-American leaders make few gestures to learn Spanish or to appreciate the unique perspectives and problems articulated by progressive Latino groups. Even Jackson's notable overtures to the Latino community in the 1988 primaries really didn't go far beyond the expression of political platitudes, without subsequent programmatic cooperation between these urban ethnic constituencies after the Democratic primaries ended.

African Americans have to recognize demographic trends and the new multi-ethnic realities. Throughout America's history until the mid-twentieth century, "race relations" usually meant black-white relations. This is no longer true. Today, one in four Americans is nonwhite.

Three decades from now, the nonwhite population will have doubled, to 115 million, while the white population's size will remain the same. But hispanics, not African Americans, will comprise the dominant ethnic group. Any progressive urban policy agenda must emphasize the many economic, educational, and social problems which Latinos and blacks share in common. Despite the perception among some blacks that the majority of hispanics are middle class or are relatively privileged, statistics show a different reality. In 1988, the Census Bureau reported that poverty rates for whites was only 10.1 percent; hispanics and blacks had poverty rates of 26.8 percent and 31.6 percent respectively.

The median family income of hispanics declined 5.7 percent between 1979 and 1988, compared to increases of 2.5 percent and 1.8 percent for black and white families respectively. According to the National Council of La Raza, as of 1988, one-half of all hispanics had not completed four years of high school, compared to one in three African Americans and only one in five whites. When factored separately, Puerto Ricans' statistics on poverty, unemployment, poor housing and education are worse than those for African Americans.

Like African Americans, Asians have experienced racial discrimination and vigilante violence. The tragic 1982 case of Chinese American Vincent Chin, who was murdered by Detroit auto workers who believed he was Japanese, was only one example of a disturbing trend. Many Asians are working class or poor. One-quarter of New York's Chinatown population in 1980 was below the poverty level. As for middle-income Asians, they frequently confront problems experienced by middle-class blacks. Most Asian professionals complain about the "glass ceiling" inside corporations and academic institutions, limiting their upward mobility into administrative ranks. The "affluent, hardworking" Korean shopkeepers, according to Takaki, have average household incomes of between $17,000 and $35,000 annually, hardly ranking with the idle rich. When Asian American families do out-earn whites, this is usually because they have more income earners per household. The reality behind the image of so-called Asian-American affluence is that there is economic and social common ground with other people of color. This is not to minimize the profound differences in languages, culture and history which separate these groups. But the foundations for coalitions nevertheless exist.

June 1990

A Strategy for Democracy: Empowerment, Leadership and Vision

Americans are frustrated and disgusted with the behavior of most politicians this year, including President Bush and the Congress. Elected officials are afraid to make difficult decisions, and seem to lack a political and even moral compass. But we should recognize that people generally get the leadership they deserve. If we look to politicians for the answers to society's problems, nothing will ever get resolved.

Three elements or characteristics are missing from contemporary politics, which used to be part of the civil rights movement of the 1960s and other democratic protest movements in our history. Any strategy for democracy which addresses the practical problems of working people must include empowerment, leadership and political vision.

Empowerment is essentially a capacity to define clearly one's interests, and to develop a strategy to achieve those interests. It's the ability to create a plan or program to change one's reality in order to obtain those objectives or interests. Power is not a "thing," it's a process. In other words, you shouldn't say that group has power, but that, through its conscious activity, a group can empower itself by increasing its ability to achieve its own interests.

This distinction is extremely important, because many progressive political movements have failed to understand the nature of power. When Congress passed, and President Lyndon Johnson signed the 1964 Civil Rights Act and the 1965 Voting Rights Act, many observers insisted that the Negro had won "power." And of course, the subsequent election of hundreds of black office hold-ers, including Virginia Governor Douglas Wilder and New York City Mayor David Dinkins, seemingly vindicated that view. But this was a misreading of what had actually happened. The civil rights movement had increased blacks' ability to achieve certain objectives, but it didn't change fundamentally their oppressed status within the economic or social system. Segregation had ended, yet blacks were not empowered to control the banks, the corporations or the government. Power is not a zero-sum game, like poker. If people of color, women or other his-torically oppressed groups gain certain rights, that doesn't mean that the system's elites actually lose any power at all. Empowerment only comes when people un-derstand what their own interests are, and develop spe-cific strategies to achieve those objectives.

Secondly, the quality of democracy depends on lead-ership, the learned ability to represent and articulate the goals and objectives of any group. Leadership isn't some-thing which people have at birth; it's learned over time, and through experiences. Leadership is acquired by plac-ing young people into responsible positions where they are forced to make hard decisions, for the benefit of the community. Leadership means being able to take a stand, regardless of the odds. These are qualities which our political system doesn't teach, but which have to be re-learned if politics ever is going to address our needs in the future.

Thirdly, the most important missing element in American politics today is vision. I don't mean some abstract or parapsychological concept here. Political vi-sion requires asking very deliberate questions, which can only be answered in the context of changing one's reality. When did the last politician you heard say something like, "What would it really take for this society to abolish unemployment, poverty or homelessness? What would it really take to attack the drug traffic in our central cities, to construct a system of mass transit, to reduce pollution, and to uproot racism and sexism?" A political vision of emancipation is more than a set of ambitious goals, it's the courage to state what's wrong with our society, and to call upon people to resolve collectively these problems.

If we want to reclaim our political system, the answer won't be found in false solutions such as restrictions on the number of years individuals are permitted to serve in Congress or the state legislatures. The real problem isn't with the politicians; it's within ourselves. Unless we rethink everything we mean by "politics," nothing will ever change for the better.

November 1990

Multicultural Democracy:
The Emerging Majority
for Justice and Peace

We can no longer regard Western Europe and North
America as the world for which civilization exists; nor can
we look upon European culture as the norm for all peoples. Henceforth the majority of the inhabitants of the
earth, who happen for the most part to be colored, must
be regarded as having the right and the capacity to share
in human progress and to become copartners in that
democracy which alone can ensure peace among men, by
the abolition of poverty, the education of the masses,
protection from disease, and the scientific treatment of
crime...[So long as] the majority of men can be regarded
mainly as sources of profit for Europe and North America...we are planning not peace but war, not democracy
but the continued oligarchical control of civilization by
the white race.

—W. E. B. Du Bois[1]

Who is the emerging new majority for justice and
peace in the United States? It consists of 31 million
African Americans, women, men and children who have
experienced slavery, Jim Crow segregation, ghettoization,
poverty, high rates of unemployment and police brutality.
It includes the Latino population, which is now projected
to reach 35 million by the year 2000, more than double the
1980 census figure. Nearly two-thirds of the Latino population is Chicano. Like their African-American sisters and
brothers, Latinos experience systemic racial and class
oppression. One-quarter of all Latino households are
below the federal government's poverty line, compared to
just 9 percent for whites. The average annual family

249

income for Chicano families is only $22,200; for Puerto Rican households, $19,900 per year. Latinos and African-Americans suffer double the rate of unemployment, and triple the rate of homelessness experienced by whites.

Who is the emerging new majority in the United States? It is the Asian/Pacific-American population, doubling in size over the past decade to more than six million people. The images of affluence and the rhetoric of the so-called "model minorities" mask the essential common ground linking Asian Americans to other people of color. The brutal murder of Vincent Chin in Detroit and ethnic harassment of Asian people throughout the country, the efforts to undercut educational opportunities and access for Asian Americans, and political maneuvers to divide and to compromise progressive political currents in Asian-American communities, link these struggles to related issues for African Americans and Latinos.

The new emerging majority are our Arab-American sisters and brothers, at least three and one-half million strong, who are subjected to political harassment, media abuse and ethnic discrimination. The FBI surveillance, interviews and intimidation aimed against Arab-American leaders during the recent U.S. blitzkrieg of Iraq parallels the forced incarceration of thousands of Japanese Americans on the west coast during World War II.

The new majority includes 2.2 million Native Americans who have been targeted for genocide by the U.S. government for more than 200 years. The struggle of American Indians is simultaneously political, cultural, and spiritual; a struggle for national self-determination and sovereignty; the reclamation of the land; and the spiritual renewal of the strength and vision of a people.

And the new majority is connected inevitably with the hopes, dreams and struggles of millions of poor and working class women and men who are white—the homeless and unemployed, the small farmers and factory workers, the students surviving on student loans, and white women with children on Aid to Families with Dependent Children. We need to keep in mind constantly that 60 percent of all welfare recipients are white; that 62 percent of all people on food stamps are white; that more than two-thirds of Americans without medical insurance are white. Racial and national oppression is very real, but beneath this is an elitist dynamic of exploitation linked to the hegemony, power and privileges of corporate capitalism over labor. There is no road for the oppressed challenging the power and the dynamics of racial oppression which does not also challenge and confront corporate capitalism.

What is the political future and prospects of this emerging majority? Before the end of this decade, the majority of California's total population will consist of people of color—Asian Americans, Latinos, Arab Americans, Native Americans, African Americans and others. And not long after the midpoint of the next century, no later than 2056, we will live in a country in which whites will be a distinct "minority" of the total population, and people of color will be the numerical majority. The next half century will be a transition from a white majority society to a society which is far more pluralistic and diverse, where multilingualism is increasingly the norm, where different cultures, religions, and philosophies are a beautiful mosaic of human exchange and interaction. *That* is the emerging majority.

What is a progressive agenda for the newly emerging majority? We have to be committed to the completion of the civil rights agenda—legislation which protects civil liberties and human rights, which advocates expanded minority set-aside programs for the development of capital formation in our communities; the passage of the 1991 Civil Rights Act which reverses six discriminatory decisions of the U.S. Supreme Court. We won't have the basis for a just society until we realize the legislative agenda of Martin Luther King, Jr.

But our responsibility is to go beyond the dream of Martin, seeking more than an integrated cup of coffee. People of color must radically redefine the nature of democracy. We must assert that democratic government is empty and meaningless without the values of social justice and multiculturalism. Multicultural political democracy means that this country was not built by one and only one group—Western Europeans; that our country does not have only one language—English; only one religion—Christianity; only one economic philosophy—corporate capitalism. Multicultural democracy means that the leadership within our society should reflect the richness, colors and diversity of our people. Multicultural democracy demands new types of power-sharing and social development for those who have been most oppressed. Multicultural democracy must mean the right of all oppressed national minorities to full self-determination, which may include territorial and geographical restructuring, if that is the desire of the oppressed nation. Native Americans cannot be denied their legitimate claims to sovereignty as oppressed nations and we must fight for their right to self-determination as a central principle of democracy.

Multicultural democracy must articulate a vision of society which is feminist, or "womanist," in the words of Alice Walker. The patterns of oppression and exploitation of women of color—including job discrimination based on gender, race and class; rape and sexual abuse; forced sterilization; harassment and abuse within the criminal justice system; housing discrimination against single mothers with children; the absence of pay equity for comparable work; political under-representation; and legal disfranchisement—combine to perpetuate this subordinate status within society. No progressive struggles have ever been won for people of color, throughout history, without the courage, contributions, sacrifices and leadership of women. No political agenda of emancipation is possible unless one begins with the central principle of empowerment and full liberation for all women of color, at every level of organization and society. Men of color must learn from the experiences and insights of sisters of color if they are to free themselves from their political, cultural and ideological chains which reinforce our collective oppression.

Multicultural democracy for the emerging new majority of people of color must embrace the struggle against homophobia, the fear, hatred, discrimination and oppression of lesbians and gay men. Homophobia is a form of social intolerance which has its most devastating impact upon people of color. By turning away from the concerns and political issues which motivate lesbian and gay activists in our communities, we construct vicious barriers between sisters and brothers, mothers and daughters, fathers and sons. We give comfort and support to the hate-filled homophobic politicians and evangelical Christian charlatans who attack lesbian and gay rights. We must recognize finally that any assault against the human dignity and personal freedoms of lesbians and gays inevitably undermines the basis for all progressive politics. When a lesbian of color is denied the right to keep her child, when a gay couple cannot adopt children, or when a lesbian is refused an apartment or job, all of us are violated, all of our rights are diminished. We must certainly build political coalitions and bridges between formations and organizations of all people of color and with specifically gay and lesbian activist groups. But we must also do much more to construct bridges of genuine support, dialogue and solidarity, challenging homophobic assumptions, homophobic policies and practices at all levels of society.

Multicultural democracy must include a powerful economic vision which is centered on the needs of human beings. Is it right for the government to spend billions for bailing out the fat cats who profited from the Savings & Loan crisis, while millions of jobless Americans stand in unemployment lines, desperate for work? Is it fair that billions are allocated for the Pentagon's permanent war economy, to obliterate the lives of millions of poor people, from Iraq to Panama, from Grenada to Vietnam, while three million Americans sleep in the streets, and 37 million Americans lack any type of medical coverage? Is it a democracy when you have the right to vote, but no right to a job? Is it a democracy when people of color have the freedom to starve, the freedom to live in housing without adequate heat, the freedom to attend substandard schools? Democracy without social justice, without human dignity, is no democracy at all.

The new majority for justice and peace must have an internationalist perspective. We must link our struggles domestically and locally with the battles for human rights and peace across the world. We are on the opposite side of the international barricades of Bush's "New World Order," which promises the "Same Old Disorder": disruption, political domination and social destruction for the third world, for working people, for the oppressed.

Multicultural democracy means taking a stand on behalf of all indigenous people, the Native Americans across the Americas, the Pacific islands, Australian, and across the world. It means expressing our political and moral solidarity with the masses of Southern Africa, the battle against apartheid led by the African National Congress, the multiracial trade union movement, and all the women and men of South Africa who are fighting for democracy.

The emerging multicultural majority must support all struggles for self-determination, and especially the people of Palestine. Despite years of brutal repression, the closure of the universities, the deliberate destruction of homes, the Intifada continues, the hope of self-determination is not extinguished, and the dream of political freedom has not died. We must learn from the courage of the Palestinian people, and extend our support and solidarity. And with this same gesture of material and moral solidarity, we embrace the masses in Central America, fighting U.S. corporate and imperialist hegemony. We find strength in the people of Cuba, standing nearly alone against the northern capitalist leviathan. The New World Order threatens the socialist revolution of Cuba, it threatens every oppressed nation and people in the third world. Our response in pressuring the leviathan, challenging the system while inside "the belly of the beast," is our unique responsibility and our cause.

Unity between progressives of color is essential if multicultural democracy is to be achieved. This doesn't mean that we minimize the difficulties inherent in such a project, the differences of perspective which exist between groups. Unfortunately, the experience of oppression does not inoculate one from being intolerant towards others. There are white lesbians and gays who are racist, and people of color who are homophobic; there are Asian Americans who are hostile to Latinos, Latinos who are hostile to African Americans, and African Americans who are prejudiced against Asian Americans. We frequently speak different languages; we have different historical experiences, religions, political ideologies and social values. But so long as these differences divide us into potentially antagonistic camps, the powers which dominate and exploit us collectively will continue to flourish. As long as we bicker over perceived grievances, maximizing our claims against each other, refusing to see the economic, political, cultural and social common ground which can unite us, we will be victimized by capitalism, sexism, racism, national oppression, homophobia, and other systems of domination. The choice is ours.

No single group has *all* the answers. No single group is embodied with all the truth. But together, the collective path to human liberation, self-determination and sovereignty will become clear.

Unity is a deliberate act of commitment, bridging the differences and emphasizing elements of common understanding. Unity must be constructed in a manner which establishes a sense of trust and shared experiences between various groups. No single group can determine all policies; no single constituency can dominate leadership; but each group must be respected and its perspectives recognized in this process.

How do we build political unity? We can begin by advocating activism which bridges differences across ethnic lines. Fighting for immigrant and refugee rights isn't a Chicano issue, or Asian-American issue, but cuts across various groups and serves our collective interests. In February, when an investigation of border violence against undocumented workers occurred in the San Diego area, participating groups included the Japanese American Citizens League, the Break the Silences on Anti-Asian Violence Coalition, Los Angeles' Project on Assault Against Women, MAPA, SEIU and UE trade unionists, and the San Francisco Black Fire Fighters' Union. Unity means building coalitions with a broad, progressive perspective.

We can construct unity by pooling our resources and energies around progressive projects designed to promote greater awareness and protest among the masses of people of color. This could mean joint mobilizations against the 1992 Columbian Quincentennial. Any "celebration" of the so-called "Conquest" of the Americas and the Caribbean is a gross insult to the millions of Native Americans, Asians and Africans who died in the expansion of capitalism, the transatlantic slave trade, and colonialism. We have the opportunity to denounce 500 years of invasion, war, genocide and racism, by holding teach-ins, demonstrations and collective protest actions. We could initiate "Freedom Schools," liberation academies which identify young women and men with an interest in community-based struggles. A curriculum which teaches young people about their own protest leaders, which reinforces their identification with our collective cultures of resistance, will strengthen our political movements. The new majority must build progressive research institutes, bridging the distance between activists and community organizers of color, and progressive intellectuals who can provide the policies and theoretical tools useful in the empowerment of grassroots constituencies.

Progressives of color on college campuses must play a decisive role in the current debate on "multiculturalism" in higher education. Ideologues of the far right—such as William Bennett, former Secretary of Education in the Reagan administration—are increasingly using higher education as the vehicle for pushing back communities of color. They've reduced student grants, attacked ethnic studies programs, undermined programs for the recruitment of working-class students and students of color, and criticized courses requiring a multicultural non-western perspective for all students. This ideological offensive against diversity and ethnic pluralism in education is the counterpart to the racist vigilante violence and harassment against people of color which is proliferating in the streets and in our neighborhoods.

What is most revealing about the intellectual bankruptcy of these conservative critics of ethnic studies, open admissions policies and multicultural diversity on campus is that their critique is silent on the actual power relationship between people of color and women, and the dominant, upper-class male elites who actually control American universities and colleges. People of color still represent small minorities of all university and college professors and administrators. The majority of white college campuses have no requirements for courses in ethnic or multicultural studies. The context for this debate occurs at an historical moment in which a conservative president vetoes a civil rights bill, the Supreme Court undermines affirmative action, and the economic and social conditions of African Americans, Latinos, and other people of color have deteriorated sharply. Therefore, to argue that people of color have the institutional means to intimidate thousands of white college teachers by demanding "political correctness," or that we have the authority to intimidate and to impose our multicultural imperatives on hapless white students, is at best grossly dishonest.

We must set the contours for the debate on multiculturalism in education, and recognize this as a central political task for the 1990s. We must assert that civilization, cultures and language patterns from South and Central America, from the Native Americans, from Africa, the Caribbean, Asia and the Pacific, have also profoundly influenced the pluralistic American experience, and the complex and contradictory identities of its people. Multiculturalism should approach each cultural tradition among people of color with an awareness of its own integrity, history, rituals and continuity. We must recognize that the perspective of multiculturalism, the struggle to create a more democratic, pluralistic educational system in this country, is part of the struggle to empower people of color, to liberate our minds from the dependency of racist, sexist and homophobic stereotypes. Such an education seeks not just to inform but to transform.

Finally, we must infuse our definition of politics with a common sense of ethics and spirituality which challenges the structures of oppression, power and privilege within the dominant social order. Part of the strength of the black freedom movement historically was the merger of political objectives and ethical prerogatives. What was desired politically, the destruction of institutional racism, was simultaneously ethically and morally justified. This connection gave the rhetoric of Frederick Douglass and Sojourner Truth, W.E.B. Du Bois, Paul Robeson and Fannie Lou Hamer, a moral grandeur and powerful vision which was simultaneously particular and universal. It spoke to the uplifting of the African American, but its humanistic imperative reached to others in a moral context.

Multicultural democracy must perceive itself in this grand tradition, as a critical project which transforms the larger society. It must place humanity at the center of politics. It is not sufficient that we assert what we are against; we must affirm what we are for. It is not sufficient that we declare what we want to overturn, but what we are seeking to build, in the sense of restoring humanity and humanistic values to a system which is materialistic, destructive to the environment, and oppressive. We need a vision which says that the people who actually produce society's wealth should control how it is used.

The moral poverty in contemporary American society is found, in part, in the vast chasm which separates the conditions of material well-being, affluence, power and privilege of a small elite from the masses of others. The evil in our world is politically and socially engineered, and its products of poverty, homelessness, illiteracy, political subservience, race and gender domination. The old saying from the sixties—we are part of the solution or part of the problem—is simultaneously moral, cultural, economic and political. We cannot be disinterested observers as the physical and spiritual beings of millions of people of color and the poor are collectively crushed.

Paul Robeson reminds us that we must "take a stand," if our endeavors are to have lasting meaning. The new emerging majority must project itself, not just as reforming the society at the edges in small ways, but project a program and vision of what should be and what must become reality. Can we dare to struggle, dare to build a new democracy, without poverty and homelessness; can we dare to uproot racism, sexism, homophobia, and all forms of social oppression? Can we dare to assert ourselves as an emerging multicultural democratic majority for peace, social justice, for real democracy? Let us dare to win.

June 1991

Notes

1. W. E. B. Du Bois, *Color and Democracy: Colonies and Peace*, Millwood, NY: Kraus-Thompson, 1975, p. v.

About the Author

Manning Marable is the most influential progressive scholar of color in the United States today. Born in 1950, Dr. Marable is Professor of Political Science and History at the University of Colorado's Center for Studies of Ethnicity and Race in America. He has written eight books, including *Black American Politics* (1985), *W. E. B. Du Bois* (1986), and *Race, Reform and Rebellion: The Second Reconstruction* (second revised edition, 1991). He is currently completing a major political biography of Malcolm X, and is also working on a study of black social protest organizations in the twentieth century, entitled *Black Liberation.* His political commentary series, "Along the Color Line," appears in over 200 publications throughout the United States and internationally. In the past decade, Dr. Marable has delivered more than six hundred lectures and speeches at college and public forums across the United States.

About Common Courage Press

Noam Chomsky once stated in *Necessary Illusions: Thought Control in Democratic Societies* that "Citizens of the democratic societies should undertake a course of intellectual self-defense to protect themselves from manipulation and control, and to lay the basis for more meaningful democracy." The mission of Common Courage Press is to publish books on the syllabus of this course.

To that end, Common Courage Press was founded in 1991 and publishes books for social justice on race, gender, feminism, economics, ecology, labor, and U.S. domestic and foreign policy issues. The Press seeks to provide analysis of problems from a range of perspectives, and to aid activists and others in developing strategies for action.

You can reach us at:

Common Courage Press
P.O. Box 702
Monroe, ME 04951
207-525-0900

Send for a free catalog!